HENRY DAVID
THOREAU

Thomas Y. Crowell Company . New York

HENRY DAVID
THOREAU

*Writer and Rebel*

BY PHILIP VAN DOREN STERN

Manufactured in the United States of America

L.C. Card 74-139108
ISBN 0-690-37715-0

1   2   3   4   5   6   7   8   9   10

CONTENTS

HENRY DAVID
THOREAU

THE EARLY YEARS

1817-1837

Walden is a perfect forest mirror, set round with stones as precious to my eye as if fewer or rarer. Nothing so fair, so pure, and at the same time so large as a lake . . . lies on the surface of the earth.

He first saw Walden Pond when he was four or five years old. It made such an impression on him then that he never forgot the small tree-lined lake with its clear greenish-blue water. The placid pond is only a mile or so from Concord where David Henry Thoreau was born on July 12, 1817. That was the name his parents gave him, but he changed it to Henry David Thoreau soon after he got out of college. The family name, incidentally, is pronounced Thúrrow in Concord.

The Thoreau family moved to Chelmsford near Lowell, then to Boston, and finally back to Concord in the spring of 1823. At that time the town had fewer than 2,000 people, and was best known because the American Revolution had begun there on April 19, 1775. Every Concord boy could tell the story of the

1

fight with the British redcoats near the North Bridge.

The first Thoreau had arrived in America just two years before that. He was a young French sailor from the Isle of Jersey, who had been on a ship commissioned as a privateer to prey on enemy commerce. The enemy commerce was British, for France and England were then at war. But Jean Thoreau was shipwrecked, and he had a miserable time until he was rescued and brought to Boston. Then he went to sea again, this time with Paul Revere, the man who was to warn Concord and Lexington of the coming of the redcoats. After the war, the founder of the Thoreau family became a store-keeper and moved to Concord.

Concord was already an old town, as American communities go, for it had been founded shortly after 1635 when the first settlers bought land from Tahttwan, the Musketaquid tribal chieftain. The Concord River was called the Musketaquid by the Indians.

In the pleasant countryside near the town, the Assabet and Sudbury Rivers come together to form the Concord River, a wide, quietly flowing stream that sometimes overflows and floods its low-lying shores. People still go fishing there and in the many ponds nearby.

Concord itself has its own watercourse—the Mill Brook which runs through the place where the Mill Dam formed a pond in Thoreau's time. The Indians had had a fish weir there, and a beaver dam may have blocked the stream even before the man-made brush fish trap was built.

When Thoreau was born, Concord already had wide tree-lined streets and fine, well-built wooden houses. Everyone knew everyone else, and most townspeople felt that it was a good place to live. It was on one of the important roads that led to Boston, which was only about 20 miles away. Down this road passed stage-coaches, oxcarts, and farmers' wagons, all adding color and excitement to the otherwise quiet country village.

John Thoreau, Henry's father, was a pencil maker at a time when pencils were just coming into use. His shop was in a small building a few hundred feet away from his house in the center of town. Everything in Concord was on a very small scale. You walked to wherever you wanted to go, and there was no hurry about getting there.

Young Henry first went to school in an old house where Miss Phoebe Wheeler taught small children. Many years later he noted in his *Journal* that he had asked Miss Wheeler: "Who owns all the land?" And when he got a medal for geography, he asked his mother: "Is Boston in Concord?"

He recorded other childhood memories—how he had been kicked by an ox, how he had caught an eel with his brother John and then went to bed with his boots and cap on. He also found a sprouted potato which he planted in his own little garden. John dug it up and put it in his garden. Then sister Helen did the same thing. Little Henry ran crying to his mother who ruled that he was the original discoverer of the potato and that it should be his. He replanted it in his plot and tended it until it produced a good crop which the family had for dinner.

Despite his independence of spirit, Henry was to be close to his mother all his life. His father was a more remote figure. But the family was a closely knit one with all four children devoted to their parents. Helen was the oldest; then came John, Henry, and last of all, Sophia.

Their mother kept a boardinghouse, so there were always people around. Since it was one of the few places in Concord where one could stay economically, Henry was to meet a number of interesting guests at the family table.

The growing boy went on to the public grammar school on the Square. There pupils of all ages sat on benches facing the teacher—the youngest in front, the older ones farther back. Each child could listen to all the lessons and perhaps profit from them.

Even as a child Henry kept pretty much to himself. John, who was far more outgoing, liked to sit on the schoolyard fence and tell stories and jokes, but Henry lacked that ability. He was studious, but his marks were not outstanding.

The fields and woods around Concord were his class-rooms, his observatories, and the places where he learned most. In them he was always at home. Many years later he said: "I remember how glad I was when I was kept from school a half a day to pick huckle-berries on a neighboring hill all by myself to make a pudding for the family dinner. Ah, they got nothing but the pudding, but I got invaluable experience beside! A half a day of liberty like that was like the promise of life eternal."

Though he liked best to be outdoors exploring the countryside, he nevertheless read widely and was advanced enough in his studies to enter the Concord Academy when he was eleven years old. Latin, Greek, and French were the important subjects there, although English grammar and spelling, history, geography, astronomy, botany, natural history, and mathematics were also taught. The instructor was an earnest and learned man, but he made a poor impression on his students. Thoreau later said of him, "I was fitted, or rather made unfit, for college at Concord Academy and elsewhere, mainly by myself, with the countenance of Phineas Allen, Preceptor." But this may have been unfair; better-than-average students always educate themselves. Their teachers can only help the basic learning process.

After Henry finished his last term at the Academy, he built a rowboat and used it to explore the waterways of Concord. Even a fairly heavy boat can be carried from place to place on a borrowed hayrick. In this way he was able to take the boat to landlocked Walden Pond and float leisurely on the waters that were later to become so important in his life.

There was some talk about apprenticing Henry to a carpenter because he was so clever with tools, but the family finally decided that he was to go to Harvard. There had not been enough money to send John to college, but the pencil-making business had improved, and it was felt that with some economy Henry could go. The cost would be $179 a year, which was then a large sum.

Henry barely passed the entrance examinations during the summer of 1833. He was allowed to enter the freshman class, but he had to make up work in Greek, Latin, and mathematics.

On August 30, he and his friend Charles Stearns Wheeler went to Cambridge where they shared a room on the fourth floor of Hollis Hall. Harvard was a small, somewhat rural-looking place of learning with a few buildings clustered around a hollow square called the Yard. Cows were driven through the unpaved streets, and farmers' wagons often rumbled by.

In Thoreau's day there were only about 250 students and 35 instructors at Harvard. The curriculum was strictly a classical one, primarily intended to train students for the ministry. The subjects taught were a continuation of those that Henry had been exposed to at the Concord Academy. But there was a good library of 50,000 books where serious students had access to the great literature of the world. Henry got most of his education in the library.

The student's day at Harvard in the 1830's began at six o'clock in the morning with prayers in the unheated chapel. Classes started before breakfast, which consisted only of coffee and hot rolls. Then came more classes until lunchtime when an adequate but not very interesting meal was served. The afternoon was less strenuous, but there was always at least one class except on Saturdays. Evening prayers at six were followed by tea, coffee, and bread. Then the students had some free time until the study hour, at eight o'clock in winter and at nine in summer, was announced by the ringing of a bell. Silence settled over the college after that. The only sounds tolerated were the scratching of pens and the rustling of turned pages. Conversation was forbidden while each student pursued his lonely way through close print, much of it in Latin or Greek.

But Harvard had its advantages for a devoted reader like Thoreau. It had one of the best libraries in America from which he could take out book after book. He not only read them but painstakingly copied many passages. Eventually there would be some five or six thousand pages in his notebooks, for he continued this practice of keeping what were then called commonplace books for the rest of his life.

Time-consuming as such work was, it did make Thoreau remember the essence of the great literature of the past. Quotations from these commonplace books were to be used in his own writings. *Walden* has many of them, and *A Week on the Concord and Merrimack Rivers* has perhaps even more.

Thoreau became a good but not a distinguished student. He had no trouble with languages, quickly improved his Greek, Latin, and French, and then went on to Italian, Spanish, and German. When the college permitted needy students to take time off in order to earn some money, he taught school for a while in Canton, Massachusetts. There he met Orestes Brownson, minister, philosopher, and original thinker. He continued his German studies with him. Eventually Thoreau became a good linguist, not in conversation but in the ability to read foreign languages.

After his return to college, the young student was compelled to stay away from his classes for months in the spring of 1836 because of illness. The records do not tell us what was wrong with him, but he may have been suffering from an early attack of tuberculosis, the disease that killed so many people in those days. It ran in his family and brought about the death of his sister Helen in 1849.

Thoreau became well enough by summertime to build another boat. He also made his first trip outside of Massachusetts, for he went to New York with his father to sell some of the pencil shop's products to stationery stores there. Then he returned to Harvard for graduation.

When one of Thoreau's classmates recalled him in later years, he said that "he was cold and unimpressionable" and that "he did not care for people." Another remarked that he "was of an unsocial disposition, and kept himself aloof from his classmates."

Yet what they said seems to be denied by his behavior during the Dunkin Rebellion in his freshman year when some of the Harvard students, angered by the rigid behavior of their Greek instructor, wrecked his classroom and broke its windows. Then, according to the official college record, "morning and evening daily prayers were . . . interrupted by scraping, whistling, groaning, and other disgraceful noises." The next evening "the Chapel bell was rung, (a cord having been attached to it,) accompanied by great noises in the yard."

We do not know whether Thoreau was one of the bell ringers, although he was to toll the Concord town bell during the fight against slavery. But we do know that he was among those questioned by the authorities when he attempted to defend a classmate who was about to be dismissed for making noise in chapel.

Although Thoreau's behavior at college was generally excellent, signs of his rebellion against authority were beginning to appear. When his fellow townsman, Ralph Waldo Emerson, wrote to President Quincy of Harvard to ask for financial help for Thoreau, the president, after paying tribute to Thoreau's good conduct, said that the otherwise well-behaved young man had "imbibed some notions concerning emulation & College rank."

This cautious phrasing was an implied criticism of Thoreau for having been one of the 38 members of his class who had signed a petition in March 1834 urging the faculty to do away with President Quincy's elaborate marking system in which credit was given for attendance in class and chapel and for oral and written work, while demerits for misbehavior lowered the students' grades.

The records show how Thoreau made out under this system. Compared with his friend Charles Stearns Wheeler, for instance, he does not rate very highly, as the table on the next page shows.

| | | Number of | WHEELER | | THOREAU | |
Year	Term	Students	Total Mark	Rank	Total Mark	Rank
Freshman	First	49	1203	12	1215	11
	Second	50	2889½	8	2629	16
	Third	51	4541	3	4038	17
Sophomore	First	46	6355½	3	6206	6
	Second	45	8115	3	7744	7
	Third	43	9920	4	9034	11
Junior	First	46	11641	2	10261	14
	Second	45	13086	2	10290	22
	Third	44	14468	4	10290	23
Senior	First	44	15999	3	11462	23
	Second	46	17050	2	12112	24
	Third	45	18179	2	14397	19

It must be remembered, however, that Thoreau had to be absent several times, first to earn a living and then because of serious illness.

These marks, of course, are in accordance with President Quincy's rating system.

During summer vacations in these college years, young Wheeler built a crude shanty on the shores of Flint's Pond near Concord. (Thoreau may have helped him construct it.) According to a friend of Thoreau's, who recalled the little hut many years later, "It was very plain, with bunks of straw, and built in the Irish manner."

Here Thoreau stayed with Wheeler for some weeks. The same friend explained that "Mr. Thoreau wished to study birds, flowers, and the Stone Age, just as Mr. Wheeler wished to study Greek."

If Thoreau was interested in the Stone Age in the 1830's, he was one of the first Americans to pay any attention to that early stage of mankind's development. Few books about it had then been published, and the few that did exist had to be obtained from Europe. But it is a tribute to Thoreau that even at that time he wanted to know more about the scientific discoveries that were just beginning to cast light on man's origins. Most Americans were satisfied with the Book of Genesis, which said that Adam and Eve were the first human beings, and that they had come into existence as fully developed, language-speaking creatures. Darwin's theory of evolution was more than 20 years ahead.

Thoreau's stay in Charles Wheeler's pondside cabin may also have had other important aspects. The idea of having a similar place of his own may very well have come from this summer with Wheeler.

On July 4, 1837, the people of Concord dedicated the monument at the Old North Bridge where American militiamen had driven off the British redcoats in the battle of April 19, 1775. For this occasion Emerson had written the now famous words:

> By the rude bridge that arched the flood,
>   Their flag to April's breeze unfurled,
> Here, once, the embattled farmers stood,
>   And fired the shot heard round the world.

It was a hot, sunny day when several military companies, followed by two or three hundred townspeople, marched down the road that led from Concord to the battlefield. After prayers and an oration, Emerson's words were sung to the tune of Old Hundred. Thoreau was among those who attended the ceremony, and he was in the choir that sang his fellow townsman's hymn.

The Battle of Concord meant a great deal to him. He had studied its details and used to seek out people who were old enough to have been eyewitnesses to the events that had taken place in those quiet meadows more than forty years before he was born.

The young man from Concord was steeping himself in local history and folklore, but his interests were expanding far beyond those limited themes. He wanted to know about the history of all places and all times. He read the literature of the world, Oriental as well as European. But his thoughts turned again and again to the problems of his own country.

There were only a few American writers then, and they found it difficult to get published. They were in competition with noted British authors, men like Scott, Coleridge, Carlyle, and two promising young novelists —Charles Dickens and William Makepeace Thackeray —whose works were just beginning to appear. Their books were pirated in America soon after they were printed in England, but the works of American authors were seldom issued abroad. "Who reads an American book?" said Sydney Smith, the brilliant but caustic British critic.

It was time for American writers to assert themselves and gain fresh confidence in their own ability. A few leaders were needed to point the way.

In those days, college customs were very different from what they are now. Commencement at Harvard was then held on the last Wednesday in August. As one of the graduating students, Thoreau spoke in a conference on "The Commercial Spirit of Modern Times." What he said on August 30, 1837, expressed a belief that he was to hold all his life:

Let men, true to their natures, cultivate the moral affections, lead manly and independent lives; let them make riches the means and not the end of existence, and we shall hear no more of the commercial spirit. The sea will not stagnate, the earth will be as green as ever, and the air as pure. This curious world which we inhabit is more wonderful than convenient; more beautiful than it is useful; it is more to be admired and enjoyed than used. The order of things should be somewhat reversed; the seventh should be man's day of toil, wherein to earn his living by the sweat of his brow; and the other six his Sabbath of the affections and the soul,—in which to range this widespread garden, and drink in the soft influences and sublime revelations of nature.

The day after the commencement ceremonies, Emerson spoke at Harvard before the Phi Beta Kappa Society and delivered one of the most timely addresses that the already ancient college yard had yet heard. It was entitled "The American Scholar," and it emphasized self-trust for the individual. Near the beginning of the long speech he said:

Our day of dependence, our long apprenticeship to the learning of other lands, draws to a close. The millions that around us are rushing into life, cannot always be fed on the sere remains of foreign harvests. [Then, toward the end, he added] We have too long listened to the courtly muses of Europe. . . . We will walk on our own feet; we will work with our own hands; we will speak our own minds.

This address, which Oliver Wendell Holmes called "our intellectual Declaration of Independence," offered much-needed encouragement to American scholars and writers who had felt that it was essential for them to be educated in Europe and make a reputation there in order to impress their fellow countrymen.

Thoreau was well aware of this problem. The year before he had written:

We are, as it were, but colonies. True, we have declared our independence, and gained our liberty, but we have dissolved only the political bands which connected us with Great Britain; though we rejected her tea, she still supplies us with food for the mind. The aspirant to fame must breathe the atmosphere of foreign parts, and learn to talk about things which the homebred student never dreamed of, if he would have his talents appreciated or his opinion regarded by his countrymen.

The young Concord student, just graduated from college, was ready to assert his independence not only from European ways of thinking but also from the traditional ways of his own country.

SCHOOLTEACHER

1837-1843

 Pens to mend, and hands to guide.
Oh, who would a schoolmaster be?
Why I to be sure

A Harvard graduate of the class of 1837 had relatively few choices of profession—the ministry, the law,
medicine, banking, or teaching. Of these, only teaching
was of interest to the young Thoreau. Teaching ran in
the family, and his older sister and brother were already
employed in the schools of Taunton, Massachusetts.

He did not have to ponder the question very long,
for he got an immediate offer to teach in Concord's
Center School where he had once been a student. The
salary of $500 a year was excellent for those times, be-
cause a depression that was to last for seven years had
started in May, and more than 600 banks throughout
the country were to fail.

He began his classroom work, but before two weeks
were out he was visited by a deacon who was a member
of the three-man school committee. When the deacon

noted that Thoreau did not punish the children for their misdeeds, he told him that "he must flog or use the ferrule, or the school would spoil." After the classes were over, the young schoolteacher chose six of his pupils by lot and ferruled them.

Before the day was over, he sent in his resignation. A few months later he wrote to Orestes Brownson about his ideas of the teacher-pupil relationship:

I would make education a pleasant thing both to the teacher and the scholar. This discipline, which we allow to be the end of life, should not be one thing in the schoolroom, and another in the street. We should seek to be fellow students with the pupil, and we should learn of, as well as with him, if we would be most helpful to him. . . . I have even been disposed to regard the cowhide as a nonconductor. Methinks that, unlike the electric wire, not a single spark of truth is ever transmitted through its agency to the slumbering intellect it would address.

This was very advanced educational philosophy for 1837 when American schools were still primitive places of instruction in which the strict discipline of the home was expected to be continued. A sleepy child was hit to keep him awake, a stupid one to make him pay attention, while a troublemaking one was severely punished to compel him to behave properly.

Word may have spread about Thoreau's unconventional ideas on education. At any rate, he found it difficult to obtain another position anywhere. Actually, he wanted to stay in his beloved Concord. Once, when he asked his mother what he should do, she, perhaps unthinkingly, said, "You can buckle on your knapsack and roam abroad to seek your fortune."

Tears came to his eyes. His sister Helen put her arm around him and said, "No, Henry, you shall not go: you shall stay at home and live with us."

During this period of unemployment, Thoreau went to work in his father's little pencil factory. Once he gave it attention, he saw that the manufacturing process used there needed improvement, for the pencils were inferior to those that came from Germany. He read all the technical literature he could get on the subject in the well-stocked Harvard Library and soon discovered that the graphite used in the German pencils was mixed with finely ground Bavarian clay. He also found out that the graphite had to be ground finer than it was in America. He devised mills and machines to do this and was able to turn out pencils that compared favorably with the German ones. Thoreau pencils became so good that they were used by artists and draftsmen.

The business expanded; more sheds were built to house it, but Thoreau lost interest because he had solved the problem. He continued his search for a teaching job, although he much preferred to be a writer.

His first published writing appeared in Concord's *Yeoman's Gazette* on November 25, 1837. It came from his interest in the American Revolution, and was an obituary of an elderly woman who had been "a connecting link between the past and the present." "Poverty was her lot," he said, "but she possessed those virtues without which the rich are but poor."

This was, of course, a very minor attempt at authorship, but Thoreau was already involved in a more ambitious project. He knew that his chances of getting anything published were slight, but there was no reason why he could not put his ideas on paper and store them away for future use. On October 22, 1837, he had begun a journal, something he was to continue for the rest of his life.

This journal, which was recorded in a series of ordinary blank notebooks, was to be the central core of Thoreau's writing career. To it he entrusted almost everything he wanted to say; from it he took most of the passages that appear in his printed works. It was a testing ground, a repository, a memory bank. A careful study of the manuscripts shows how much he drew upon his journal when he sat down to write.

Diaries and journals are often begun—especially by young people—but their writers usually lose interest in what soon becomes a chore. A journal, of course, is easier to keep than a diary, for entries do not have to be made every day, and there is no feeling of guilt at the sight of long blank spots. In fact, a journal has no blank spots; one entry follows another no matter how much time has passed since the previous one was made.

This casual form suited Thoreau perfectly. He could fill page after page with the details of one day's experience—or the thoughts inspired by it—and then let time go by until he had something else worth writing about.

Although he does not mention Emerson's name, it was probably he who suggested that Thoreau start a journal. He began his lifelong work with this brief statement: " 'What are you doing now?' he asked. 'Do you keep a journal?' So I make my first entry to-day."

And then he went on to say: "To be alone I find it

necessary to escape the present,—I avoid myself. . . .
I seek a garret. The spiders must not be disturbed, nor
the floors swept, nor the lumber arranged."

One might assume that a carefully kept journal would
give us minute details about the events of Thoreau's life.
But he was not that kind of journal-keeper. He was
more interested in ideas, thoughts, dreams, musings
about his inner life, and observations about nature, literature, friendship, and love than he was about himself or
about current events.

The published *Journal*, which is printed in 14 volumes, contains nearly a million words, but it tells very
little about Thoreau as a citizen of Concord or of the
United States. Yet it gives us an amazing amount of
information about him. Thoreau is supposed to have
been a reticent person, but his *Journal* reveals his inner-
most thoughts.

The winter passed, and spring came on. On March 17,
1838, he wrote to his brother John suggesting that they
go west together on a canalboat trip. It was said that
there were plenty of teaching jobs to be had in Ken-
tucky. They were all set to leave in April when word
came that there was a position open in Alexandria,
Virginia. The western trip was postponed, but the
teaching post in the South never materialized.

Since he seemed to be getting nowhere in teaching,
he tried lecturing, probably inspired by Emerson's success in that field. It is hard to think of Thoreau as a
public speaker, for the short, plain-looking, plainly
dressed, little-traveled country boy from Concord had
none of the attributes of a popular lecturer. He was

completely serious; he refused even to attempt to amuse
his listeners; he spoke in a low, rather monotonous
voice; and he usually had a poor opinion of his audiences. Fortunately we have most of his speeches. Their
content is good; what he had to say was important. It
was the way he spoke that detracted from their value.

Emerson was a successful lecturer who often went on
long speaking tours. On the platform he had everything
that Thoreau lacked. He was gracious and friendly. His
training as a minister had given him a great deal of experience in handling an audience. He knew what his
listeners wanted and did not want. And he could tell
when they were getting restless. Thoreau, however,
was not out to please his audience and often said so in
his *Journal*.

He gave his first lecture in Concord's Masonic Hall
on April 11, 1838. The subject was "Society," something
he liked to talk and write about all his life. The entries
he had already made in his *Journal* on March 14 give
us some idea of what he told his audience that evening:

The mass never comes up to the standard of its best member, but . . . degrades itself to the level of the lowest. . . .
The field of battle possesses many advantages over the
drawing-room. There at least is no room for pretension or
excessive ceremony, no shaking of the hands or rubbing of
noses. . . . It . . . exhibits one of the faces of humanity, the
former only a mask.

Despite these harsh judgments, the lecture was a success, which encouraged Thoreau to go on in that field
although he was never to become a really good speaker.

Later that year he was elected secretary and then cura-
tor of the Concord Lyceum, positions he was to retain
for several seasons. Getting speakers to lecture in Concord brought him in contact with some outstanding people and bolstered up his failing opinion of himself at a
time when things were not going well.

In the early nineteenth century, long before motion
pictures, radio, and television were invented, people had
very little to entertain or instruct them. They would
pay to go to a lecture, especially during the long winter
nights when there was very little to do. Out of this
situation came the lyceums. They began in 1826 and
soon became so popular that there were several thousand
of them. Each one was intended to be a cultural center.
Concerts—mostly vocal—were held in them, but they
were primarily for lectures. Emerson was very successful with lyceum audiences; so were James Russell
Lowell, Henry Ward Beecher, Horace Greeley, Margaret Fuller, and British speakers like Dickens and
Thackeray. Famous people were most in demand, but
even a relatively unknown lecturer could go from one
town to another and make a living, even though the
fees for such a speaker were quite small.

Concord's Lyceum was founded in January 1829 and
did so well that during the following fifty years it
brought nearly a thousand lectures, debates, and concerts to the town. It was an important cultural influence, which educated people were glad to support and
encourage.

Thoreau knew that it would take years for him to
become established on the lyceum circuit. Meanwhile,

he continued to concentrate his efforts on getting work as a schoolteacher.

Since the Concord Thoreaus had relatives in Bangor, Maine, the would-be schoolteacher decided to visit them and also go to some of the other towns in that state. He started out on May 2 on the steamship that ran between Boston and Portland. This was his first encounter with open water, and he soon found out that he was a poor ocean traveler, for he became miserably seasick. (It may have been this that discouraged him from ever going to Europe.)

He spent some time with his relatives in Bangor, visited a number of Maine towns, and talked at length with an elderly Indian about woodlore and Indian customs. The Maine wilderness and the Indians made so great an impression on Thoreau that he was to return there several times and write about that most northern New England state. But no schoolteaching work was available. It was too late in the season; hiring for the next term had been completed.

After he returned to Concord, he kept trying, but he had no luck. In June he started his own school, using one of the rooms in his father's house for the students. Those coming from out of town could board with the family. During the summer, when the headmaster of the Concord Academy resigned to take a better position, Thoreau was able to rent the building, use the Academy name, and continue the work of that school.

At first the new establishment did not do well, but before long so many students were enrolled that it became possible for brother John to give up his post in

Roxbury and return to Concord to teach in the Academy. With his greater experience he took charge, and the school soon began to flourish.

The Thoreau brothers ran the Academy on principles that were very advanced for the time. Pupils who wanted to enter had to promise to devote themselves to their studies and not waste time. If they agreed, then the Thoreaus would do their best to teach them. Each week the boys were taken for walks in the woods or fields, for a sail on the river, or for a swim in one of the ponds. In the spring of 1839 the two brothers built a larger boat which they named the *Musketaquid*—the Indian word for the Concord River, meaning "grass ground." It took them only a week to build it. According to Henry's description, their new boat was shaped

like a fisherman's dory, fifteen feet long by three and a half in breadth at its widest part, painted green below, with a border of blue, with reference to the two elements in which it was to spend its existence . . . and was provided with wheels in order to be rolled around falls, as well as two sets of oars, and several slender poles for shoving in shallow places, and also two masts. . . .

Henry had great interest in Indians and used to tell his pupils about the people who had lived on the Concord land before Europeans settled there. He pointed out probable sites for their villages and sometimes was able to uncover the fire-blackened stones that had been their fireplaces. He had a special gift for finding Indian relics and could pick up arrowheads where no one else saw them lying half-hidden in the soil.

The boys were also introduced to the more practical aspects of American life by being taken to the local newspaper office to see the type set and the big sheets printed. A visit to a gunsmith shop showed them something about fine tools and their use, while the elements of surveying were taught in the field. Gardening also was part of the curriculum even though other schools ignored such manual work. Some of the townspeople must certainly have disapproved of these novel teaching methods. But they worked; boys in the Thoreau school did very well, and their friends begged their parents to be allowed to go there.

Henry was an even greater innovator than John. When one of the students asked him a question he could not answer, he candidly said so and promised to find out the information. He did not forget the inquiry; as soon as he had the answer, he would tell the class what he had discovered.

The students thrived under such teaching; they liked and respected their instructors and enjoyed being with them. They were never punished. The usual recess of ten minutes was lengthened to half an hour for play and exercise, and the windows were opened to ventilate the classrooms while the boys were outdoors. This meant that more fuel had to be burned in cold weather, but the brothers thought that the fresh air was worth it.

In June 1839 eleven-year-old Edmund Sewall came from Scituate to Concord for a visit. He must have been an attractive young lad, for Thoreau wrote a poem dedicated to this "Gentle Boy." Then, when Edmund's seventeen-year-old sister Ellen visited Concord in July, both Henry and John fell in love with her. They had always been very close; now they wanted the same girl.

Evidently Ellen Sewall was a very charming young lady. Her visit to Concord lasted only two weeks, but during that short time she managed to make a lasting impression on the Thoreau brothers as well as on several other young men of the town. During her visit Henry wrote in his *Journal*, "There is no remedy for love except to love more."

On the last day of August 1839, the two brothers set out on a river trip that was to be immortalized in Henry's first book. They were going to explore the Concord and Merrimack Rivers, which would take them well into New Hampshire.

Their new boat, the *Musketaquid*, would carry them, and it would also be their sleeping quarters. One of the masts could be used as a tent pole, while a buffalo skin would be their bed.

It was a quiet voyage. They passed farmhouses and forests, went under bridges where the pickerel could be seen lying attentively in the shadows, saw fishermen and lock-tenders, slept at night in their tent, and sometimes picked up Indian relics when they went ashore. They had left on a Saturday and did not encounter rain until Thursday when they were well past Manchester. They left their boat with a farmer and went ten miles on foot to Concord, New Hampshire, where they stayed with friends.

The next day they took the stagecoach and traveled on it until they were in sight of the White Mountains.

Leaving the stage, they explored the rock-strewn water-courses until they got to Profile Lake where they could see the huge, naturally formed face on the cliffs that is called the Old Man of the Mountains.

What they really wanted to do was climb to the top of Mount Washington. It was their first experience with high places. The summit is 6288 feet above sea level, and from it they got a spectacular view of all New England. Then they started back, picked up their boat, and arrived home two weeks after they had set out.

Soon after their return from the river trip, John went to Scituate to visit Ellen Sewall. Then, at Christmas, both brothers went to see her. Henry began to write poems addressed to her. During the spring, her brother Edmund became a boarding student at the Thoreau school. In June, Ellen came to Concord for a brief visit.

While she was there, Henry took her out on the river and wrote in his *Journal*:

The other day I rowed in my boat a free, even lovely young lady, and, as I plied the oars, she sat in the stern, and there was nothing but she between me and the sky. So might all our lives be picturesque if they were free enough.

Soon after Ellen returned to Scituate, John went there to see her. This time he proposed marriage, and she accepted. Her mother quickly made her break off the engagement because the Thoreaus were known to be "too modern" in their religious thinking to suit Ellen's strict father.

Henry apparently thought that the way was now clear for him. But Ellen's parents sent her to stay with relatives in upstate New York. When he wrote a letter of proposal of marriage to her in November, her father insisted that she refuse. She did so, and the matter ended there.

Ellen married a young minister named Osgood in 1844 and went to live with him in Cohasset, Massachusetts. Henry remained friendly with the married couple and sometimes stopped off to visit them when he was in that part of the state.

During the winter of 1840–1841, John Thoreau's health, which had never been very good, got steadily worse. Tuberculosis, which ran through the family with deadly persistence, was claiming him. He was losing weight and tired easily. It was obvious that he could not continue to teach, and the Thoreau school, which had shown so much promise, was closed at the end of March.

Nor was Henry well during this winter. He came down with an attack of bronchitis which kept him confined to the house for several weeks in February. *Journal* entries made during this month show that he was thinking of renting or buying land somewhere near Concord. The idea of having a house at Walden Pond can be traced to these early thoughts. On April 5, a few days after the school had to close, he wrote in his *Journal:* "I will build my lodge on the southern slope of some hill and take there the life the gods send me."

The one thing that Henry Thoreau was to be most

interested in all his life was writing. He knew that he would never make any great amount of money from it, but his need to communicate his ideas to others had to find an outlet. He wanted to be a poet, but before long he found out that he was able to express himself better in prose.

At this time a new philosophical and literary movement called Transcendentalism was attracting many American writers. The basic ideas for the movement had originated in Germany and were carried to England by the writings of Coleridge and Carlyle. From there they crossed the ocean and took root in America, largely in New England.

The word "Transcendentalism" indicates what the movement means, that there is something born in man that is essentially good and that it *transcends* the senses. Children therefore are naturally good and may fall from grace only because they are influenced by the man-made evil around them. The Transcendentalists believed that intuition, in critical moral judgments, was superior to reason; that the individual was all important; that kindness, consideration, and love were more powerful in influencing people than the bullet or the sword. The practical businessmen and political rulers of Thoreau's time, of course, thought that such ideas were radical nonsense. And he himself was eventually to come to the realization that this might be a harsher world than the one the Transcendentalists so earnestly believed in.

Leading exponents of Transcendentalism were Emerson, Orestes Brownson, Bronson Alcott, and Margaret Fuller. Brownson, of course, was the brilliant but somewhat erratic scholar with whom Thoreau had boarded and studied German during his college years. Alcott, peddler, poet, visionary, and writer, is now better known as the father of Louisa May Alcott, author of *Little Women*, than he is for any of his own works. Highly intellectual young Margaret Fuller became the editor of a new literary magazine called *The Dial* which was the mouthpiece of the Transcendentalist movement. Thoreau could therefore hope to have his work published in it, for he was a Transcendentalist who was very close to Emerson, the most prominent and influential of them all.

One barrier, however, was the editor, Margaret Fuller. Everyone in Concord knew this brilliant woman, but she was a strong individualist who was determined to print only material that appealed to her. Thoreau was lucky enough to have a poem and a short essay on a Latin poet published in the first issue. He had nothing in the second one, and Margaret Fuller, after a delay of five months, rejected his next article. She did accept some of his poems, however. When she resigned as editor in the spring of 1842, Emerson took over her post. Thoreau then had his first long piece dealing with Nature published. It was entitled, "Natural History of Massachusetts."

In the winter of 1842–1843, Emerson was so busy with lectures that he asked Thoreau to produce the April 1843 issue of *The Dial*. In it the temporary editor placed several things of his own. When Emerson returned, he printed Thoreau's "A Winter Walk" and several other pieces. *The Dial* did not pay for material, but while it lasted it was an outlet for Thoreau's work. Unfortunately it ceased publication in April 1844, after printing only 16 numbers.

The circulation of *The Dial* was less than a thousand, yet it played an important part in the development of American literature. Its standards were high; its editorial taste usually impeccable; but it never aroused enough public interest to become commercially successful; and, like many other ambitious journals of its kind, it could not continue. Nowadays copies of it are collector's items.

The Dial published a number of poems, translations, and essay-type book reviews by Thoreau, a total of 31 pieces. "Natural History of Massachusetts" was supposed to be a review of some scientific reports on the plants, invertebrates, insects, fish, reptiles, birds, and quadrupeds of the state. Thoreau did not think much of the publications and gave them slight attention. Most of his article is about his own experiences in the fields and woods of Concord and is thus a foreshadowing of *Walden* even in style. So is the other *Dial* nature essay, "A Winter Walk." And as he often did, he inserted some of his own poems in the articles in order to get them printed.

The Thoreau poems that appeared in *The Dial* are as good as any he was ever to write, which means that they are in no way remarkable. This man, whose best prose work approaches the emotional level of fine poetry, was never at home with verse. He wrote most of it in his youth and then stopped. He produced enough, however, to make a full-length book.

A third review, a brief notice of an Abolitionist weekly, the *Herald of Freedom*, published by Nathaniel P. Rogers in New Hampshire, is really a publicity notice for that worthy paper. Thoreau wanted to bring it to the attention of sympathetic readers of *The Dial*.

At the end of the school year, Thoreau had no work to do—and no income. He was glad to get odd jobs, some of them of the kind that many would spurn. He notes in his *Journal* that one day he earned 75 cents for heaving manure out of a pig pen. He was never proud and considered no manual labor beneath him, although he thought it was a waste of time for a man who had better things to do. "Great thoughts hallow my labor," he said of the pen-cleaning task.

Emerson came to his rescue before the month was over. Thoreau was to live in his fine, big home and earn his board and lodging by working a few hours a day on the house and its grounds. Emerson, who had already helped Thoreau while he was in college and who had encouraged him as a writer, was now to become an even closer influence. For a while he would be an authority figure. But with a fiercely independent young man like Thoreau that was an invitation to trouble.

LIFE WITH
THE EMERSONS

1841-1843

I was amused by R. W. Emerson telling me that he drove his own calf out of the yard, as it was coming in with the cow, not knowing it to be his.

Ralph Waldo Emerson was fourteen years older than Henry Thoreau, a difference in age that might make him seem like an elder brother but not really like a father. He was good-hearted, generous, and wise, but he made the mistake of treating Thoreau more as a son than as a younger brother.

Emerson's family had come from Concord, but Emerson was born in Boston, and he served there as a Unitarian minister in the early part of his life. He was following a family tradition, for many of his ancestors had been ministers. In 1829 he married young Ellen Tucker. Her family had a history of tuberculosis, to which she also succumbed two years later when she was only nineteen.

Emerson had been very much in love with his pretty young wife. Her death had a profound effect upon him, but it was only one of the causes that were making his inquiring mind question the doctrines of the church. "How little love is at the bottom of these great religious shows; congregations and temples and sermons—how much sham!" he wrote in his journal. As to the ministry, he noted, "The profession is antiquated. In an altered age, we worship the dead forms of our forefathers."

Emerson retired from the pulpit before the end of 1832 and left Boston on a ship bound for the Mediterranean. He traveled from Italy to England and was greatly impressed by the evidences of civilization, ancient and modern, that he saw there. He met Coleridge and Wordsworth but at a time when they had both become querulous old men who were only shadows of the great poets they had been in their youth. Thomas Carlyle, however, was still young—only eight years older than Emerson—and the brief time the two men spent together was the most memorable experience in Emerson's visit to Europe. He returned home, arriving there in October 1833. A year later he moved to Concord, boarding for a while with his stepgrandfather, Ezra Ripley, in the famous Old Manse that overlooks the battlefield.

He knew the ancient house well, for he had often visited it. On a wood panel alongside an upstairs fireplace was an inscription put there by his father in 1780. In 1824 his brother Edward had added another, while he himself had written below the two records: "Peace to the Soul of the blessed dead. Honor to the ambition of the living."

While still boarding at the Old Manse, Emerson

married Lydia Jackson of Plymouth, a rather plain-
looking, pleasant woman who was eight months older
than he. (Emerson was now thirty-two.) He persuaded
his wife to change her name from Lydia to Lidian
because he thought that Lidian Emerson sounded better
than Lydia Emerson.

Like Thoreau, Emerson had graduated from Harvard,
had taught school, and also had tuberculosis in his family.
He was not rich, but he had inherited some money from
his first wife, and he added to it by traveling around
the United States to speak on all sorts of subjects from
natural history to art, philosophy, and literature. He
also earned a small income from his books.

Shortly after his marriage to Lidian he bought a
house at the edge of the village—and on the side toward
Walden Pond. It was a large frame building with many
rooms, enough for the four children he was to have and
also to give him a good-sized library and study. At the
top of the front stairs was a small bedroom that was to
be Henry's.

It is not known just when Henry Thoreau first met
Emerson, but it must have been shortly after Emerson
moved to Concord. Henry was still in Harvard then,
and while he was there, he got a new insight into his
fellow townsman's mind when he read Emerson's first
book, *Nature*, soon after it was published in 1836.

This seemingly simple and very short book had a
great influence on the young Thoreau. He had always
loved the woods and the fields and plants and animals
of all kinds, but Emerson's *Nature* told him more about

their inner meaning than he had ever known before. In addition to everything else, the book summed up the essentials of Transcendentalism and served as a good introduction to that difficult subject. The publication of *Nature* in fact helped to bring the Transcendentalist movement into being, for two weeks after it appeared, Hedge's Club (named after one of its members) was informally founded. Emerson, naturally, was among those present. So were such distinguished men as Bronson Alcott, Orestes Brownson, George Ripley, and James Freeman Clarke.

The little 96-page book was a plea for solitude, for a return to Nature where man might find peace, a chance to meditate, and thus rejoin God. Not matter but spirit, the book said, was the foundation of man. Each one of us is "part and parcel of God."

Emerson had a still further influence on the young man he had taken into his home. In addition to everything else, the house had a fine library. At last Thoreau had on hand the books he had long wanted to read. He was particularly pleased to find texts on Oriental philosophy and religion. Others might be repelled by the heavy-looking tomes with their contents as hard-going as their exteriors implied, but Thoreau welcomed them and plunged into the abstract wording of such translations from the Sanskrit as *The Laws of Menu* and the *Heeto-pades of Veeshnoo-Sarma*. Of Menu (now spelled Manu) he said, "They are the laws of you and me, a fragrance wafted down from those old times, and no more to be rejected than the wind. . . . I remember the book as an hour before sunrise."

Oriental philosophy appealed to Thoreau because it emphasized the nonmaterial aspects of life. He realized that the American culture of which he was a part was growing more and more materialistic every day. Wealth, property, and possessions were what counted in Concord where a man was rated by what he owned rather than by what he was.

Hindu philosophy showed that the great thinkers of ancient India were men of soaring imagination. To them, man and his world were only minute parts of a vast concept in which time and space fell away and became nothing. There were no straight lines in their superuniverse. Everything was curved; everything turned around and repeated itself, not as it was, but in ever-new guises, always advancing upward until the transformed being reached Nirvana and was absorbed into its forever blessed silence.

These were strange ideas for a young Concordian to have, for the little village was still a country place far removed from the ideas of older civilizations. But Thoreau had been to Harvard, had used its great library, and now had access to Emerson's books and Emerson's mind.

The Emerson home was an ideal place for so intellectual and thoughtful a young man. And Lidian, the mistress of this house of learning and culture, was a sympathetic figure to whom Thoreau could always look up as if she were his sister—or perhaps his mother. He got on well with the small Emerson children, too. They were glad to have a companion who could do all sorts of tricks and answer any question they might ask.

It was while he was at the Emersons' that Thoreau

was asked to serve as tutor to Richard Fuller, who needed some special instruction to prepare for Harvard. He was the brother of brilliant Margaret Fuller, editor of *The Dial.* During the summer the two young men went on a four-day trip to Wachusett Mountain, 25 miles west of Concord, traveling all the way on foot. The journey was described by Thoreau in an article the *Boston Miscellany* published in January 1843. The magazine was supposed to pay him, but it never did.

Emerson and Thoreau got on well, especially when they worked together around the house and its gardens. The older man was notoriously clumsy with his hands —"my imbecile hands," he called them—but Thoreau was a true jack-of-all-trades who could literally do anything with his. There is no doubt that the Emersons had the better of the bargain, for clever, honest, and hard-working young people are always hard to find for doing menial jobs.

Before long, Emerson was writing to England to Thomas Carlyle that "one reader . . . of yours dwells now in my house—and, as I hope, for a twelve-month to come,—Henry Thoreau,—a poet whom you may one day be proud of—a noble, manly youth full of melodies and inventions. We work together day by day in my garden."

At the end of the first summer with the Emersons, Thoreau put a note in his *Journal* which shows that the basic idea for *Walden* was already stirring in his mind:

I think I could write a poem to be called "Concord." For argument I should have the River, the Woods, the Ponds, the Hills, the Fields, the Swamps and Meadows, the Streets

and Buildings, and the Villages. Then Morning, Noon, and
Evening, Spring, Summer, Autumn and Winter, Night,
Indian Summer, and the Mountains in the Horizon.

An examination of *Walden* will show how this fore-
shadows the form and contents of that book. It has
chapters on the village, the ponds, and the surrounding
fields and woods, while the seasons run all through it
with a special chapter on the coming of spring. But the
finished product has much more, for Thoreau put into
it his philosophy, his reactions to the society in which
he lived, and a great deal about himself. The projected
poetic form was abandoned, which was fortunate, for
Thoreau never expressed himself well in verse. In its
stead, the superb prose structure of *Walden* took shape
over a period of nearly ten years. But this entry in the
Journal and the final wording of *Walden* show how
closely Thoreau was attached to the small bit of Massachusetts that was his native ground.

Early in January 1842, the pleasant lives that the
Thoreaus and Emersons were leading were suddenly
interrupted by tragedy. While stropping his razor, John
Thoreau made a minor cut on the tip of one of the
fingers of his left hand. He bound it up and paid little
attention to it until it began to swell up and fester. Then
he got medical treatment, but doctors did not yet know
about germs and viruses. He had lockjaw (tetanus), a
disease that was prevalent when horses and farm animals
roamed the streets. It rapidly became worse, and within
a few days he was mortally ill. Henry had returned

from the Emersons' house to take care of his brother. He watched over him day and night, but there was no stopping the onslaught of the terrible disease. John died on January 11.

For several days after the funeral, Henry sat in his father's house not wanting to speak to anyone. Then, eleven days later, he began to show symptoms of the same illness. But the affliction was what doctors now call psychosomatic. He did not have lockjaw, but his mind, overcome by the sudden loss of his beloved brother, was acting out the way he had died. Henry had no control over what he was doing; he had to relive his brother's suffering. And he did. Gradually he got well, but he could not leave the house for more than a month. Even then he was depressed and silent for a long while.

Matters were not helped by what was happening in the Emerson home. There five-year-old Waldo got scarlet fever and died of it on January 24. Thoreau had known the little boy well and was very fond of him. Death seemed rampant that winter in Concord. On February 21 he wrote in his *Journal:* "I feel as if years had been crowded into the last month."

Eventually he returned to the Emersons' house, and spring came to erase the traces of that sad winter.

The Emerson home had much more interesting visitors than Mrs. Thoreau's simple boardinghouse. Many were intellectuals from Boston and places even farther away. At this early period, however, Emerson's house had not yet evolved into the shrine it was to be when he became internationally known. Yet the men and women who came there even during the early 1840's gave Thoreau a chance to meet people whose minds he could respect.

Emerson was a great help to the young writer who was still trying to find his way. Thoreau's chief outlet was *The Dial*, but he was writing an article that was soon to be published in the *Boston Miscellany*. This was the nature piece, "A Walk to Wachusett."

Then, on July 8, 1842, an author moved into the town whose presence was to add literary distinction to Concord. This was Nathaniel Hawthorne, who, with his young bride, Sophia Peabody, took over the Old Manse. His *Mosses from an Old Manse* made the house forever famous. In 1842, however, Hawthorne had published only two books: a little-known novel, *Fanshawe*, and *Twice-Told Tales*. Yet he was very much the professional author whose life was dedicated to writing.

Thoreau had made the Old Manse ready for the Hawthornes, and he came to see them soon after they arrived. At first, the two men had little to say, and what they did say was said in short, mumbled phrases. But the Hawthornes invited Thoreau to a dinner at which he evidently made enough of an impression on Hawthorne for him to put down this account:

Mr. Thorow [*sic*] . . . is a singular character—a young man with much of wild original nature still remaining in him. . . . He is as ugly as sin, long-nosed, queer-mouthed, and with uncouth and somewhat rustic, although courteous manners, corresponding very well with such an exterior. But his ugliness is of an honest and agreeable fashion, and becomes him much better than beauty.

All those who knew him agree that Thoreau had a prominent nose ("more like a beak," one of his friends said). According to his own account, he was "about 5 feet 7 inches in height—of a light complexion, rather slimly built"—and, as everyone, including himself, freely admitted, utterly indifferent to clothes. He bought the cheapest and sturdiest garments that would give the longest wear for the money they cost, and then he would use them until they were no longer able to hold together.

Deep-set blue eyes, brown hair, a determined mouth, and a steady, even stride like an Indian's, complete the description of the man the Hawthornes entertained at dinner.

Later in the day Thoreau took Hawthorne out on the river in the boat that had carried him and his brother to New Hampshire in 1839. Hawthorne was favorably impressed with the way Thoreau handled it. Thoreau then offered to sell the boat to him for seven dollars with rowing lessons included. The deal was made, and the new owner changed the name from *Musketaquid* to *Pond Lily*. It may be that the boat had unhappy memories for Thoreau. At any rate, he was not sorry to be rid of it.

During the winter, when the river froze over, Emerson, Hawthorne, and Thoreau would go skating. Hawthorne's daughter later wrote that her father "moved like a self-impelled Greek statue, stately and grave," that Thoreau, who was obviously the best skater, performed "dithyrambic dances and Bacchic leaps on the ice," while Emerson, as befitted his greater age, "closed the line, evidently too weary to hold himself erect, pitching head foremost, half-lying on the air."

That Thoreau should be so active and vigorous a skater is not surprising. When he was well, as he was most of the time this year, he was capable of a great deal of muscular exertion. And his coordination was excellent. He liked to dance—but always solo—to sing popular songs, and to play the flute.

He was fond of music, but since he had little opportunity to hear it, his taste was untrained. His favorite song was a country piece called "Tom Bowline," and he was greatly impressed by one of the few concerts he ever attended. But he was at his best when he improvised music on his flute, often playing it at night while out in his boat.

His long stay at the Emersons' house was ending, and he sent them a gracious letter of thanks on January 24, 1843, to express his gratitude. He was getting restless, so he asked Emerson to try to find him work as a tutor.

Fortunately, Emerson's brother William needed someone to instruct his three young sons at his home on Staten Island. The arrangement was to be similar to the one Thoreau had had with the Emersons—board and lodging in exchange for work. Since he would be away from home and in an unfamiliar area where he could not hope to earn extra funds, he would also be given $100 a year as pocket money.

STATEN ISLAND

1843

I have hardly begun to live on Staten Island yet, but ... I carry Concord ground in my boots and in my hat,— and am I not made of Concord dust?

The entrance to upper New York Harbor is the narrow passage of water between Brooklyn and Staten Island. It has been an exciting place ever since the first Europeans, Giovanni da Verrazano and Hendrik Hudson, saw it centuries ago.

William Emerson's long, brown-painted house, with wide verandas and grape arbors, was located on a hill. From it Thoreau could walk down to the beach, or, even better, stand on the heights and watch the endless procession of ships pass up and down the Narrows. Those arriving from distant ports could be spotted far out at sea as their tall masts rose slowly above the horizon. And there were all kinds of smaller vessels coming and going through the passage to or from the bay.

Some were steamers, usually with side-paddle wheels, but most were sailing vessels, square-riggers, or schooners. There were even forerunners of the famous Yankee clippers, which would soon carry towering clouds of canvas for greater speed that would take them to China in 92 days.

The Narrows, then as now, was an important place for American shipping. The Quarantine Station, needed for detecting communicable diseases on incoming ships, was on the Staten Island side. So was the telegraph for notifying New York of arrivals. Since this was just before Samuel F. B. Morse's magnetic telegraph came into use, a signal telegraph transmitted the arrival notices visually by moving long arms mounted on masts.

The William Emerson household, however, was far less interesting than its surroundings. Emerson's brother was a rather ordinary person who spoke openly against Transcendentalism and other ideas that Thoreau held dear. And his three sons were very young. Only seven-year-old Willie was ready for a tutor; the other two were still toddlers. The work was hardly inspiring for a young man who had associated with the best-educated men of Concord and Boston.

Thoreau would get up early and take his pupils out before the rest of the family was awake. He could not go on long walks with such little children, but he did explore the neighborhood with them and even took them fishing on the bay. When he landed the boat one day, he brought it into a shallow place where the tide was falling so rapidly that a horse had to drag the stranded boat off the flats.

When he could be alone, Thoreau was able to walk inland to see the very old Huguenot farmhouses there, or to go on foot along the beaches where he could pick up fascinating sea drift and watch the ships go by.

Yet he was homesick from the moment he arrived on Staten Island. An impartial observer might think that the sea-girt isle would be more interesting than the simple countryside around Concord, but when Thoreau wrote to Lidian Emerson, he said: "I carry Concord ground in my boots and in my hat,—and am I not made of Concord dust? I cannot realize that it is the roar of the sea I hear now, and not the wind in Walden woods."

Anyone less firmly linked to Concord might have enjoyed the stay in Staten Island, for it was easy to get to New York from there by ferry, and Thoreau says that he went some 20 or 30 times during the summer. He was fascinated by the crowds, but he did not like the city. "The pigs in the street are a very respectable part of the population," he wrote to Emerson. (Pigs then roamed the streets of New York as many travelers have reported.)

But he did visit the bookstores where he could browse for hours on end even though he had very little money to purchase anything. The Society and Mercantile libraries were hospitable to him and permitted him to take out books. When he went to call on some of the great publishing houses like Harper's, he found that they had no use for an unknown young writer from a New England village who had only a few things from *The Dial* to show them.

Emerson's letters of introduction made it possible for Thoreau to meet some interesting people in New York. One of them was Horace Greeley, the journalist, who immediately recognized Thoreau's true worth and took a paternal interest in furthering his career. Since Greeley knew many of the publishers and editors of the magazines of the day, a word from him recommending a manuscript meant a great deal. Before long he was taking an active part in inducing various periodicals to publish—and pay for—the young Concord writer's articles.

That does not mean that Thoreau was able to make a living from his published work. He would never be able to do that. Nevertheless, he continued to write even while he was unhappy on Staten Island. Two prose pieces were published in *The Democratic Review* this year. One was "The Landlord"; the other a book review entitled "Paradise (to be) Regained."

Perhaps the change from an inland climate to the damper seacoast affected Thoreau's lungs. He caught a bad cold as soon as he arrived, and this developed into what he called bronchitis—a serious enough case to keep him confined to the house for a while. But what he called "bronchitis" may have been an outbreak of the tuberculosis from which he was never entirely free. During this time he became sleepy and remained so for months.

Despite his illnesses, he managed to get around, especially to New York. He would walk from the Battery, where the Staten Island ferry landed, to Washington Square, two miles away, and then perhaps go on to Fifteenth Street where some of his newly made acquaintances lived. The city had been laid out as far as 149th Street, but most of the upper reaches were still undeveloped. The Croton water system had just been installed with a big reservoir at Fifth Avenue and Forty-Second Street, where the Public Library now stands, but except along Broadway, which had been a main thoroughfare for more than a century, the upper part of the city had few buildings of any consequence. "There are woods all around," Thoreau wrote to his parents.

But life downtown was picturesque. Carriages and carts of all kinds, horse-drawn omnibuses, and peddlers' wagons were everywhere. Street vendors roamed through the city, crying their wares as they passed stores and houses.

Thoreau saw all this as he went through New York on foot. So did another young writer, Walt Whitman, who was living in Brooklyn and often took the ferry from there to Manhattan. He loved the many-sided, sprawling city and often said so in his poems. Eventually the two men, who had so much in common, were to meet. But that was after they had published books and were beginning to become known. In 1843 both were obscure.

In June word came to Thoreau from Germany that his friend and Harvard classmate, Charles Stearns Wheeler, had died in Leipzig, where he had gone to study. Such news, of course, only added to Thoreau's homesickness and feeling of depression.

He spent much of his free time during the summer exploring Staten Island. He went to see the Telegraph Station, the old seamen's home at Sailors' Snug Harbor,

the ancient elm trees that marked the place where the
French Huguenots had landed, and he visited village
after village, all of them as small and rural as if they had
been in the countryside near Concord. And just as he
had done on his native ground, he was able to pick up
arrowheads from the Staten Island soil.

He was interested, too, in watching the many immigrants from Europe as they arrived at the Quarantine
Station. He saw them washing their clothes and exercis-
ing while the children ran races or played "on their
artificial piece of the land of liberty" during the day or
two that their ships were being inspected and cleaned.
Then they were taken to the Battery.

When he wrote to his mother he described some of
the immigrants:

Norwegians who carry their old-fashioned farming tools
to the West with them, and will buy nothing here for fear
of being cheated—English operatives, known by their pale
faces and stained hands—Whole families of immigrants
cooking their dinner upon the pavements . . . each and all
busily cooking, stooping from time to time over the pot
and having something to drop into it, that they may be
entitled to take something out. They look like respectable
but straitened people, who may turn out to be counts when
they get to Wisconsin—and will have their experience to
relate to their children.

They would be going not only to Wisconsin but all
over the northeastern states. Some—the Irish especially
—would settle in Concord and in the towns around it
where their sturdy muscles and skill at digging were
needed.

Early in August he wrote a letter to his mother which shows how attached he was to his family—and how homesick he was for them:

I fancy that this Sunday evening you are poring over some select book. . . . Father has just taken one more look at the garden, and is now . . . reading the newspaper quite abstractedly, only looking up occasionally over his spectacles to see how the rest are engaged, and not to miss any newer news that may not be in the paper. Helen has slipped in for the fourth time to learn the very latest item. Sophia, I suppose, is at Bangor; but Aunt Louisa, without doubt, is just flitting away to some good meeting, to save the credit of you all.

Thoreau spent so much time in the fields and woods of Staten Island that some people who lived there thought he might be a surveyor. One of them hinted that he was probably well acquainted with land values, that "he kept pretty close," and that although no surveying instruments could be seen perhaps they were hidden away in his pocket.

Since Thoreau did become a surveyor later in life, it is possible that this experience in Staten Island influenced him to take up that profession seriously.

Emerson wrote to him from Concord to say that the railroad line from Boston to Fitchburg was rapidly being built and that it was to pass along the western shore of Walden Pond. Irishmen were doing the work for fifty or sixty cents for a long day of hard labor with pick and shovel. And with new job-seekers constantly arriving, competition from them would bring wages down still further.

Worries about money were affecting Thoreau also. He was trying to sell subscriptions to the *American Agriculturist* in the upper parts of Manhattan Island where there were still plenty of farms. But he was not cut out to be a salesman and did not do well enough to pay for the shoe leather he wore out. He complained to Emerson that the market for writing in New York was poor and that some of the magazines were overwhelmed by contributions from amateurs who only wanted to see their words in print and gladly offered to forego payment of any kind. Meanwhile he continued to search the papers for advertisements for schoolteachers. It is obvious that his tutoring job at the William Emerson house was not turning out well.

He returned to Concord for Thanksgiving and lectured there a few days afterward on Homer, Ossian, and Chaucer. The sight of his native town, his family, and his friends made him decide to give up his tutoring work in Staten Island.

He went back in December to collect his belongings and wind up his affairs. He had been away from home for seven months, time for the seasons to change from spring to winter. He knew now that he wanted to live in his beloved Concord and nowhere else. Except for a few short trips he was never to leave it.

CONCORD

1843-1845

The vitals of the village were the grocery, the barroom, the post-office, and the bank; and, as a necessary part of the machinery . . . a bell, a big gun, and a fire-engine.

The Concord to which Thoreau returned in December 1843 was changing more rapidly than it had during the previous half century. The iron rails that would bring the snorting steam monster to town were being laid, and in May, Samuel F. B. Morse would send his first magnetic telegraph message, "What hath God wrought?" from Washington to Baltimore. Before long the telegraph wires would reach Concord, where Thoreau was to be endlessly fascinated by the humming music they made when the wind caused them to vibrate. Both new inventions were to bring places closer together. The United States, expanding toward the West, was growing larger, yet its people were becoming less isolated.

During the winter Thoreau again went to work in

his father's pencil factory. And again he devised better ways to make the pencils. Because of his skill with tools and machinery, he could have become an engineer. But he wanted to be a poet, a writer, and nothing else. He knew how difficult such a career would be, yet he was prepared to make the financial sacrifice for it.

Concord in winter, when heavy snow blanketed the town and all the countryside around it, became a shut-in place. People seldom ventured far from home, and those who did used snowshoes or horse-drawn sleighs. Cold and difficult as such weather was, it nevertheless had its charms. The town was at its most beautiful then with clean white snow covering the mud of the streets and roads. Smoke curled from the chimneys; the clomp-clomp of axes resounded as men and boys chopped up wood for the ever-hungry fireplaces and the new patent cast-iron stoves.

But life outside the town, except for the few animals that could curl up in their hideaways and sleep through the winter, went on as usual. Thoreau would get up early to see the footprints in the snow and to watch the birds as they came out for the slender pickings that could be had during the sparse winter months.

The spring of 1844 was an unusually dry one. The rivers were running low, and last year's grass and weeds were brittle and highly inflammable.

At the end of April, Thoreau went on a fishing trip with Edward Hoar, the son of the richest man in town. Although they intended to be away for several days, they were hardly out of sight of Concord before they had enough fish for lunch. They stopped on the eastern shore of Fairhaven Bay, a wide part of the Sudbury River about two miles south of Concord, to cook their meal on an old stump by the edge of the water.

A good woodsman like Thoreau should have known that one has to keep a close watch on a fire in such dry weather, but apparently he was careless that day. The west wind, blowing across the open stretch of water, carried a burning bit of tinder to some dry grass and set it ablaze. Before they saw what had happened, the flames had spread and were running up a hill covered with tall grass and bushes.

They tried to beat out the fire with their hands and feet and then with an old board from the boat, but it quickly got away from them. Soon it was racing toward the woods.

Ed Hoar was terrified. "Where will it end?" he asked.

"It may reach the town," Thoreau said. "We'd better get help."

Ed ran to the boat to row to Concord. Thoreau started out on foot, running as fast as he could. The flames spread rapidly, and a dense pall of smoke rose into the sky.

Thoreau met a farmer leisurely driving his team down the road. "What's the smoke from?" he asked.

When Thoreau told him, he said, "Well, it's none of my stuff," and casually drove on.

Then Thoreau met the man who owned the field where the fire had started. With him, he hurried back to the burning woods.

The landowner quickly sized up what was happening and decided to run into town for help. Thoreau was winded and had to slow down. He realized that the fire was beyond anything he could do to stop it, for the front of the advancing flames was now half a mile wide.

He walked on slowly to Fair Haven Cliff and climbed up to its highest rock. From there he had a good view of the leaping flames and billowing smoke. Then he heard the town bell in Concord toll. People would soon be on their way to do what they could.

At that moment Thoreau's attitude toward what he had done suddenly changed. It took him six years to confess to his *Journal* just how he felt that day. Then he wrote:

Hitherto I had felt like a guilty person,—nothing but shame and regret. But now I settled the matter with myself shortly. I said to myself: "Who are these men who are said to be the owners of these woods, and how am I related to them? I have set fire to the forest, but I have done no wrong therein, and now it is as if the lightning had done it. The flames are but consuming their natural food. . . . I . . . stood to watch the approaching flames. It was a glorious spectacle, and I was the only one there to enjoy it.

This reasoning may seem odd in a man who loved the outdoors, advocated conservation, and opposed any kind of destruction. But Thoreau was a complicated person who sometimes came up with strange ideas. Shortly after this entry in the *Journal* he wrote down precise instructions for controlling forest fires. At the end of it he said that "the men who go to a fire for entertainment . . . are boys to be dealt with."

Whatever he may have thought of what he did that day there is no doubt about his fellow townsmen's reactions. He said in his *Journal* that they called him a "damned rascal" and that some of them kept shouting "burnt woods" for years afterward.

During the previous year, Thoreau had made a friend, the only male companion who was to be close to him now that his brother was dead. This was William Ellery Channing, Jr., nephew and namesake of the noted Boston minister. Ellery Channing and his wife Ellen had moved to Concord in the spring of 1843, and Thoreau had found a house for them just before he left for Staten Island. The house was on the Cambridge Turnpike next to Emerson's garden. Now that they were expecting a child, they were moving to a larger and better place on the Lexington Road.

Channing, in his way, was almost as odd as Thoreau. He considered himself a poet, but he wrote very little verse. He had gone to Illinois to live in an isolated cabin, had tired of it, and had returned to the East. One thing he managed to do was avoid responsibility. He was charming, witty, learned, and honest enough, but he was completely and utterly selfish. His world began and ended in himself.

He had come to Concord because he admired Emerson, but now he was finding that preoccupied sage rather remote. Thoreau, unsocial as he was, was easier to get along with. Since Channing liked to explore the woods and fields he found Thoreau the ideal companion for long walks.

During the summer of 1844, they went on a long trip. Thoreau started out ahead and met Channing in Pittsfield, Massachusetts. Together they visited the Catskills, and then took a steamer to go down the Hudson River and return to Concord.

This was the first time the two men had a chance to observe each other under all kinds of circumstances. Channing noted that Thoreau "had no shirt collar . . . and looked as if he had slept out in the fields as he was unshaved and dressed very poorly." Thoreau had spent the night in a roughly built observatory on Mount Greylock where he slept under some boards to keep warm. He had learned this trick from poor Irish children who "inquired what their neighbors did who had no door to put over them in winter nights."

On the way down the Hudson, Channing was rather annoyed to see Thoreau walking on the deck munching a loaf of bread. Despite Channing's reactions to his unconventional companion's dress and behavior, they still got on well. Since Channing was to be Thoreau's first biographer, it was good that he was able to observe his subject's idiosyncrasies and also his indifference to what people might think.

On the day they returned to Concord, an antislavery fair was being held in the corridors of the courthouse. Although many—perhaps most—of the people of Massachusetts were opposed to slavery, there were some who preferred to ignore the problem and not have it discussed in public. As a result, all the churches had self-righteously closed their doors to the fair and refused to allow their bells to be rung to publicize the event. Thoreau was particularly concerned because Emerson, who had never denounced slavery from a public platform, was to speak on this occasion. And it was a special occasion, the tenth anniversary of the day when the 700,000 slaves in the British West Indies had been set free.

When Thoreau found out that no bells would be rung to attract attention, he went to the First Parish Church, in which he had been baptized but which he had refused to join, and pulled the bell rope vigorously. A crowd soon appeared, and Emerson had a good-sized audience for his speech.

The subject of slavery was coming out into the open. The conservative people of Concord still wanted to close their eyes to it, but the intellectual leaders of the town—Emerson, Thoreau, Hawthorne, Alcott, Channing, and others—refused to keep quiet. The great issue that was to tear Concord apart—and then sunder the whole nation—was to dominate the American scene for a score of years.

During the autumn of 1844, Thoreau's father bought a building lot in the western end of Concord very near the railroad line that had recently been run through the town. The new home was on Texas Street and therefore became known as the Texas House. Texas was very much in the news then, for annexation of that state was being debated in Congress during this year and the next.

Thoreau and his father intended to build the house themselves. Before they started the construction, Thoreau excavated the cellar and lined it with stones. Then they began to erect the frame and cover it with boards. Thoreau, who was already a good carpenter, was getting added experience that was soon to prove useful.

THE CABIN
AT WALDEN POND

1845-1847

*I went to the woods because I wished to live delib-
erately, to front only the essential facts of life, and see if I
could not learn what it had to teach, and not, when I came
to die, discover that I had not lived. . . . I wanted to live
deep and suck out all the marrow of life.*

Emerson, who often used to walk from his house
to Walden Pond, bought 15 acres near the northwest
corner in 1844. The land there was largely cutover
woods and briars.

Channing went to New York that autumn to work
for Horace Greeley and the *Tribune*. In the spring he
wrote to Thoreau:

The hand-writing of your letter is so miserable, that I am
not sure I have made it out. If I have it seems to me that
you are the same old sixpence you used to be, rather rusty,
but a genuine piece.

I see nothing for you in this earth but that field which
I once christened "Briars"; go out upon that, build yourself a hut, & there begin the grand process of devouring
yourself alive. I see no alternative, no other hope for you.

Eat yourself up; you will eat nobody else, nor anything else.

Channing's advice, by itself, would probably not have been enough to induce Thoreau to leave his father's house and build a dwelling place of his own. But it helped him to decide. His *Journal* shows that such an idea had been growing in his mind for a long while. And the time was ripe for such a move. Accidentally setting fire to the Concord woods had made him even more than ordinarily unpopular with the local people. And his thoughts may have turned back to the pleasant summer he had spent with Charles Stearns Wheeler on the shores of nearby Flint's Pond. Now that he wanted more than ever to write, he had lost an outlet for his articles when *The Dial* ceased publication. He was eager to try his hand at longer works, at books. Ideas for two of them were already shaping up. One was to be about the long boat trip he had taken with his beloved brother in 1839; the other was to be based on Concord, Walden Pond, his own life, and his own thoughts.

There was no question that he knew how to go about building a house. His work on his father's new home had proved that. The one he planned to construct would be much smaller and simpler—a one-room cabin to shelter one person.

Undoubtedly there were still other reasons for what he was about to do. Some of them perhaps were deep in Thoreau's unconscious mind. It was spring, and he was restless. His restlessness called for action. Late in

March he got Emerson's permission to build on his
Walden Pond land; then he borrowed an axe, and began
cutting down some of the tall pine trees that grew
there.

The site he chose was on a gentle slope about 200
feet from the shore of a small cove. From the spot
where his little house was to stand he could look
through the trees to the pond, which was still covered
with ice. Off to his right was the newly built railroad
line that connected Boston and Fitchburg. A cut
through a hill there offered a short and easy way to
walk to the western part of Concord where the Texas
House was located. Higher up on the hill, above his
cabin site, was a cleared field which he intended to
plant with beans. And just beyond it was the narrow
road that ran from Concord to the nearby town of
Lincoln.

He had chosen a relatively isolated place, but it was
by no means a wilderness. He could hear and see the
trains go by, walk into town—or to Emerson's house—
in less than half an hour, and from the beanfield, where
he was to spend much time, converse with those who
were on their way to Lincoln or Concord.

Trains had begun running on the railroad less than a
year before, so the sound and sight of them were still
novel to local people. The puffing engines and the little
cars they drew were to make an enormous difference in
their lives. The steam engines were slow, and the cars
were primitive, but travel by rail was many times faster
than by stagecoach. Telegraph wires would soon be
paralleling the railroad track. The modern world was

making inroads even at Walden Pond. And Thoreau stood at the crossroads between the ancient ways of the past and the industrialized future.

In less than a month, although he was characteristically in no hurry, he had the exterior of his house framed and ready to be raised in place. He had already dug the cellar and put piles of flat stones in position to serve as foundations. The chimney was to come later; it was to be outside the rear wall and therefore could be built after the house was finished.

Early in May, ten of his neighbors came to the site to help raise the house. Some of them, like Emerson, were poor mechanics, but others—the farmers especially —knew from long experience just what to do. Using long poles to push the upper parts with, they put up the framework and the roof. The completion of the work was an occasion that was usually celebrated by feasting, for it meant symbolically that mankind had on that day acquired another dwelling place in which to live.

The rest of the work Thoreau could do himself, and he took his time doing it. He would carry his lunch with him, and while he ate it, he would read the newspaper in which it was wrapped. He also had to plant his beans and vegetables—two and a half acres of them. He hired a horse to plow, harrow, and furrow the field. This cost $7.50 and was one of the biggest expenses of his house-building and food-raising venture. He said candidly that it was "too much."

His other large outlay of money was $4.25 for the shanty of an Irishman who had helped to build the railroad and who now had to move on in search of other work. As soon as he and his family vacated their dwelling, Thoreau took it apart, board by board, carefully drawing the reusable nails, staples, and spikes, one by one. He took his lumber in a cart to the side of the pond and spread it out in the sun so the crooked boards would "warp back again." While it was lying there, another Irishman came along and helped himself to all the painfully salvaged hardware. Thoreau had to purchase new nails and hinges in town. This was an added expense, for they cost him more than $4.00.

Before putting on the boards, he built the foundations for the chimney, carrying big flat stones up from the pond in his arms. As soon as the house was boarded and roofed, it became a shelter from the wind and the rain. He could do his cooking outdoors until the chimney was ready.

On July 4, 1845, Thoreau moved into his still-unfinished cabin. He used a hayrick to bring his few pieces of furniture to his new abode. He described them in *Walden* as "a bed, a table, a desk, three chairs, a looking-glass three inches in diameter, a pair of tongs and andirons, a kettle, a skillet, and a frying-pan, a dipper, a wash-bowl, two knives and forks, three plates, one cup, one spoon, a jug for oil, a jug for molasses, and a japanned lamp." There were also some books, an inkstand and pen, and surely some paper, for writing was to be his chief occupation in the quiet woods around Walden. Certainly he did not expect much company; the two knives and forks indicate that.

July 4 was an important occasion. He said in his *Journal* two days later:

I wish to meet the facts of life—the vital facts, which are the phenomena or actuality the gods meant to show us—face to face, and so I came down here. Life! who knows what it is, what it does? If I am not quite right here, I am less wrong than before.

And then, on the next day, he wrote:

I am glad to remember to-night, as I sit by my door, that I too am at least a remote descendant of that heroic race of men of whom there is a tradition. I too sit here on the shore of my Ithaca, a fellow-wanderer and survivor of Ulysses.

Evidently he was enjoying those first days in his new house, for on July 14 he said:

Sometimes, when I compare myself with other men, methinks I am favored by the gods. They seem to whisper joy to me beyond my deserts, and that I do have a solid warranty and surety at their hands, which my fellows do not. I do not flatter myself, but if it were possible *they* flatter me. I am especially guided and guarded.

It was at this time that Thoreau met a young Canadian woodchopper named Alek Therien. He was a prodigious worker and a true expert with the axe, yet he had heard of Homer, and Thoreau quotes him as saying "if it were not for books, [he] would not know what to do on rainy days." Therien was a simple man, generous, outgoing, and completely a part of his natural surroundings—the forest where he worked. He was a good shot, too, and could get all the meat he wanted by hunting game. But he somehow felt that cutting wood was his trade and that that was what he should do.

Since Thoreau had to work at finishing his house and also at hoeing his beans every day, he had even less time for reading and study than he had had at home. It was essential to have the cabin ready before winter set in, so he bought a thousand second-hand bricks, laboriously chipped off the rock-hard old mortar, and built his fireplace and chimney. Then he shingled the exterior of the house. One more thing remained to be done and that was to plaster the interior walls. He did this from November 12 to December 6, which is far too late in the year for such work, for there is danger then that the wet plaster may freeze. He did not stay in the cabin during the plastering but went home to sleep and returned each day.

At last he had "a tight shingled and plastered house, ten feet wide by fifteen long, and eight-feet posts, with a garret and a closet, a large window on each side, two trap doors, one door at the end, and a brick fireplace opposite." With the lumber that was left over, he built a small shed at the rear for his firewood.

The total cost, not including his own labor, was just $28.12½, as Thoreau's carefully kept accounts show.

While the house building was still going on, he had to tend his beanfield. Although much physical labor was involved—and woodchucks ate a good part of his crop —he nevertheless made a profit of $8.71½ on an investment of $23.44. And he had, of course, more beans than he could eat.

Actually, he did not like beans, so he traded most of

them for rice, which he much preferred. It seemed to be a more suitable food for him, he said, because he "loved so well the philosophy of India." During the two years he lived in the cabin his food cost him only 27 cents a week. It consisted mostly of "rye and Indian meal without yeast, potatoes, rice, a very little salt pork, molasses, and salt." On at least one occasion he ate roast woodchuck. He was not a true vegetarian, but he generally shunned animal food. Fish were always to be had for the catching, but he disliked the mess connected with cleaning and preparing them. Sometimes he cooked edible wild plants like purslane or groundnuts. He was always fond of boiled corn and wild apples. His requirements for food were so simple that when asked what dish he preferred, he said, "The nearest."

Yet this man, who lived on a Spartan diet while he was at Walden, could criticize the cooking in his mother's boardinghouse. While he was still living there, he said that the "kitchen cabinet" was "concocting some indigestible compound" and that the pudding was unusually bad that day.

From what he says, it is evident that he had enjoyed building his house. And he also liked working in his garden until the unending need to keep down the growing weeds discouraged him. He had planted what he estimated to be seven miles of bean rows, more than one man (who had other things to do) should be asked to take care of. As a result he was not sorry when the woodchucks ate up a quarter of an acre of his crop.

He worked barefoot in the two-and-a-half–acre field,

chopping away at weeds that seemed to grow back as soon as he had cut them down. The rows were 250 feet long, and hoeing them every day was wearisome labor. He was glad when occasional passers-by on the road to Lincoln stopped their horses to talk with him. Their remarks were usually critical—that he had planted his beans too late, that corn was a better crop, why was no fertilizer being used? and other comments and questions that would occur only to professional farmers who immediately saw that they were dealing with an amateur. But much as he said that he preferred to be by himself, Thoreau apparently welcomed these intrusions on his solitude. Yet nothing anyone could have said would have made so stubborn a young man change his mind even about practical farming, a field in which he had had very little first-hand experience.

Aside from the monotony of the labor involved in hoeing the long bean rows, Thoreau resented the time the work was taking from his writing. He had built his house and come to Walden Pond to write—not to raise farm crops. The beans were supposed to supply food for the body; meanwhile his mind was being starved. He did not even have enough time to read. His japanned lamp could not have given much light, and after working in the field from 5 A.M. until noon and then doing other things afterward, he was tired and had to go to sleep early.

Raising beans was a mistake, although he was reluctant to admit it. The cash profit of $8.71½—plus some food—was not enough to repay him for the time lost and the labor spent. He resolved not to plant any vegetables the next year but to devote himself to writing instead.

The first writing Thoreau did at Walden was a long critical article on the work of Thomas Carlyle. Carlyle was admired by the Transcendentalists, and Emerson maintained a regular correspondence with him, so Thoreau was kept well posted about what the noted Scottish-born author was doing.

Like Thoreau, Carlyle was an unconventional person, stubbornly so in fact. And, like Thoreau, he was a dedicated writer who believed that his work was the most important thing he could do. Again like Thoreau, he was a man of new ideas—sometimes startlingly new ones. The fact that Emerson had met him and often talked about him doubtless influenced the young Thoreau. Since Carlyle was at the height of his power at this time, with *Sartor Resartus, The French Revolution, Heroes and Hero-Worship,* and *Past and Present* all published in one decade, his recent work was well worth writing about. Thoreau felt that American readers should be made aware of what this remarkable man had to say, and he wanted to bring him to their attention.

In his essay, Thoreau said that "Carlyle alone, since the death of Coleridge, has kept the promise of England." And from the article he was able to get enough material for a lecture which he gave in Concord early in February 1846.

Since Thoreau wrote about Carlyle in the mid-1840's, when the Scottish writer was only part way through his long career, he naturally could not foresee how this master of the vehement phrase was to become more and more antidemocratic. In later years Carlyle wrote biographies of such autocratic rulers as Oliver Cromwell and Frederick the Great; he came to the defense of Edward John Eyre, the governor of Jamaica, who had put down a slave rebellion there with what many people thought was an excessive display of force. Carlyle also wrote a tract against the 1867 Reform Act in England and in 1871 supported the German invasion of France. Some of these reactionary tendencies might have been detected in his earlier writings, but Thoreau apparently did not notice them.

The Carlyle essay was the first fairly long piece of prose for which Thoreau was paid. He was luckier with it than he was to be with many of his later articles, for Greeley sold it for him to *Graham's Magazine*, where it appeared in the March and April 1846 issues. Greeley had to bring pressure on Graham's to pay, but eventually Thoreau got his money.

Meanwhile, he settled down to the work he had come to Walden to do. This was to create a book out of the many *Journal* entries he had made about the boating trip to New Hampshire with his brother. But he was not satisfied to confine himself to the journey alone; he put in all kinds of odds and ends, thoughts about friendship, Christianity, life in general, and a great deal about books, most of them old classics. The story of the week on the Concord and Merrimack Rivers is there, too, but sometimes the daily adventures are lost in a maze of speculation. He evidently thought that a book manuscript was a good place for bits of prose he had not been able to use elsewhere, so he inserted them here and there in the growing pile of pages.

Despite its rambling form, the *Week* has its charms. And it does tell a lot about Henry David Thoreau. No one interested in his writings will want to miss it, for it serves as a sort of stepping stone to *Walden*.

Thoreau began work on *Walden* while he was still living in his cabin by the pond, but he did not get very far with it. At this time he wanted to have *A Week on the Concord and Merrimack Rivers* published. He soon found out—as most young writers do—that getting a publisher for a first book is exceedingly hard. But Hawthorne was helping him, and even though the older writer was not yet well known, his third book, *Mosses from an Old Manse*, was being issued. When he wrote to a publisher who wanted another book from him, he recommended Thoreau although he described him in words that were more than candid:

There is one chance in a thousand that he might write a most excellent and readable book; but I should be sorry to take the responsibility, either towards you or him, of stirring him up to write anything. . . . He is the most un-malleable fellow alive—the most tedious, tiresome, and intolerable—the narrowest and most notional—and yet, true as all this is, he has great qualities of intellect and character.

Thoreau did not have his manuscript of *A Week* completed at this time, but in the spring of 1846 he had Emerson write another letter to the same publisher.

Kindhearted Emerson's letter was all praise, and the publisher, after reading the manuscript, told Thoreau that the house was willing to issue it, but at Thoreau's expense.

The book then went to publisher after publisher without success. Thoreau called back the manuscript and spent another three years revising it.

Meanwhile, he was also doing other things. He kept making entries in his *Journal,* many of which were later to be incorporated in his books; he investigated the abandoned house sites of former Concord inhabitants; and he paid tribute to Alcott and Emerson in notes in his *Journal.* Of Bronson Alcott he said: "The most hospitable intellect, embracing high and low." And of Emerson: "His personal influence upon young persons [is] greater than any man's. In his world every man would be a poet, Love would reign, Beauty would take place, Man and Nature would harmonize."

Life went on quietly in the little cabin at Walden Pond. The lonely writer there sometimes had unexpected company. One of the field mice that were living under his house became so friendly that Thoreau described the little creature in *Walden:*

[It] would come out regularly at lunch time and pick up the crumbs at my feet. It had probably never seen a man before; and it soon became quite familiar, and would run over my shoes and up my clothes. It could readily ascend the sides of the room . . . like a squirrel, which it resembled in its motions. At length, as I leaned my elbow on the bench one day, it ran up my clothes, and along my sleeve, and round and round the paper which held my dinner, while I kept the latter close, and dodged and played at bo-peep with it; and when I at last held still a piece of cheese between my thumb and finger, it came and nibbled at it, sitting in my hand, and afterward cleaned its face and paws, like a fly, and walked away.

Many people attest to Thoreau's remarkable ability to get on with wild animals. A mother partridge recognized the cabin as a friendly place and would lead her chicks past it without fear. Thoreau said that he had held the little birds in his open hand where they would stay quietly until he put them down to await their mother's summons. Emerson said of him: "He knew how to sit immovable, a part of the rock he rested on, until the bird, the reptile, the fish, which had retired from him, should come back, and resume its habits, nay, moved by curiosity, should come to him and watch him."

During the winter, when food was scarce, birds came to eat the crumbs he scattered at his door, and one was bold enough to alight on an armful of wood that he was carrying toward the cabin. The squirrels became so tame that they would run across his shoes.

He explored the snow-covered fields and drifted woods, watching for muskrats, owls, foxes, and the birds that stayed in Concord all winter. The frozen pond was an especial attraction to him. He could skate on it when it was free from snow, and even when it was covered with a white blanket, it served as a short cut to places that in warm weather were a long walk around the lake.

The pond was so deep that local people called it

bottomless. Thoreau wanted to sound it, so he cut holes
in the ice and fathomed the depth by a stone tied to
a long codfish line. He found that it was just 102 feet
deep at the deepest part, although he knew that this
would vary from time to time as the water in the spring-
fed pond could rise and fall five feet or more. Modern
scientific sounding methods, incidentally, have confirmed
the figure that Thoreau established early in 1846. He
also surveyed the pond and made a detailed map of it.

He often watched fishermen come there in winter to
catch pickerel. They would cut a series of holes through
the ice about 75 or 80 feet apart, tie the upper end of
the line to a stick placed across the opening, and put the
slack in the line over an alder twig with an oak leaf
fastened to it. Then, when a fish took the bait, the twig
would be pulled up as a signal to the fisherman. He
would dash out from the shore to haul up his catch and
then return to the fire that he and his companions had
built to keep warm. There he could wait in reasonable
comfort for another fish to strike.

Thoreau usually spent his mornings at his desk, writing with a quill pen or sometimes with one of the newer
ones that had a steel point. His handwriting gradually
grew worse as his fingers tried to keep pace with his
racing thoughts. At Harvard he had written a beautiful
copperplate script; now his rapidly scrawled lines were
becoming so illegible that printers were to complain that
they could not make them out.

It was cozy on those winter mornings in the little one-
room cabin with its neatly plastered walls. The fireplace

sent out a cheerful glow; light poured in through the two windows; while the man bent over the desk wrote on and on, not noticing the mice that sought food and attention, and not even hearing the sound of the birds that were becoming more numerous as spring approached.

The ice showed signs of melting; water was running in little rivulets from patches of snow; and the sun was growing warmer each day. The red squirrels living under the house were getting restless. The man at the desk could hear them chuckling and chirruping. When he stamped his foot on the wooden floor to silence them, they became defiant and made even louder scolding noises. They were reminding him that the woods did not belong to a human newcomer but to the animals that had lived there since time began. He recognized their rights just as he conceded the rights of the woodchucks which had eaten his beans. He wanted only to be part of the vast natural scheme that was taking place around him, to understand it better in order to love all living things more.

And then he heard the first sparrow of spring. With that magic sound the long winter was officially over, even though there would be ice on the pond for weeks to come.

It had been a profitable winter. The ever-growing pile of manuscript on the desk was witness to that. Now a new season was shaping up with hopeful promise for a beginning writer who was eager to see more of his work in print.

TO JAIL FOR
CIVIL DISOBEDIENCE

1846-1849

I could not but smile to see how industriously they locked the door on my meditations, which followed them out again without let or hindrance, and they were really all that was dangerous.

As the weather grew warmer Thoreau carefully observed certain natural phenomena that most people never notice. These were the strange shapes that the sand and clay on the slopes of the railroad cut assumed as they thawed. The sand flowed like lava, and as it ran down it took on the form of leaves, coral, leopards' paws, birds' feet, and the insides of animals. He said that he felt as if he were "in the laboratory of the Artist" while "he was still at work . . . strewing his fresh designs about," and that the sand shapes were "an anticipation of the vegetable leaf."

Then he watched the wild grasses come forth, fresh and green, to replace the dry, withered growth of the year before. He was always impressed by the renewal of life; that theme runs through all of his work.

He would walk through the railroad cut to the village, and often as he had seen Concord it never failed to have novel aspects for him. Its vitals "were the grocery, the bar-room, the Post Office, and the bank" and the streets were so arranged that "every traveller had to run the gauntlet, and every man, woman, and child might get a look at him." Some people welcome human contact and look forward to meeting friends, townsmen, and even strangers, but Thoreau did not; his shyness made it hard for him to talk about the weather, health, and the state of things in general.

The spring of 1846 was a difficult time in Concord. Texas had been admitted to the Union at the end of the previous year, and trouble with Mexico was brewing along the border there. By May there was open warfare. Then California broke away from Mexico and briefly became a republic; in July the United States proclaimed possession of that Pacific Coast territory. Troops were marshaled for the war with Mexico, and the nation moved toward conquest.

Since Abolitionists felt that such a war would give more territory—and more power in Congress—to the proslavery South, men like Thoreau were naturally opposed to it. Yet many of the townspeople supported the war even when they were not in favor of slavery. "The Government knows best," they said. "And we must help the President."

The issue made tempers flare and language become violent. Northerners who had been willing to tolerate slavery now felt that the slaveowners were becoming more and more aggressive in seeking greater power in

the national government. But not all Northerners felt
that way. Some of them sold merchandise to Southern
markets and purchased cotton, tobacco, and naval stores
from Southern states. They believed that the founding
fathers who had written the Constitution were wise, and
since they had condoned slavery, the entire country
should put up with it.

Few people, North or South, would come out openly
to say that slavery was a good thing, but a great many
felt that despite its many obvious drawbacks it was a
necessary economic system suited to the peculiar needs
of the South. They thought it was regrettable that several million black people had to live as slaves, but of
course they were nothing but uneducated and unam-
bitious semisavages who were obviously suited only for
physical labor. Perhaps someday a time would come to
free them and improve their lot.

Nevertheless, resentment against slavery was growing
in the 1840's, and ardent Abolitionists were speaking
forcefully against a system they considered wrong.
Slavery, they said, was a moral issue, one that tran-
scended economic needs or legal justification. Even in a
little Northern town like Concord the feeling, pro and
con, was running high. The hangers-on who frequented
the Mill Dam were all for the war and the President
and therefore had no use for Abolitionists like Thoreau.

As a result of the war talk, he was finding it even
more unpleasant than usual to walk past loiterers who
leaned against a building with their hands in their
pockets while they made loud comments about people
with unpopular political opinions. Some of them prob-

ably knew that Thoreau not only opposed the war but that he objected to paying taxes to maintain what he called "the unjust government which makes the war."

But by walking boldly past the Mill Dam boys while he kept his "thoughts on high things," Thoreau managed to stay out of trouble with them even though he was the butt of their jokes.

Then, one afternoon late in July, when he went to the village to join a huckleberry-picking party and also to get a shoe that was being mended, he met Sam Staples, the town constable and jailer, a man he knew well and liked.

As a protest against a government that permitted slavery to continue, Thoreau had refused to pay his poll tax for six years. He knew that he was in arrears, and he also knew that Sam Staples was keenly aware of it. The political situation had changed now. A man who did not pay his taxes might be tolerated by a government in peacetime, but now that there was a war on, the matter had become serious. Delinquent taxpayers had to be reminded that their taxes were overdue.

Staples was a mild man. He quietly asked Thoreau to pay his taxes. The amount was trivial. But Thoreau shook his head.

"I'll pay your tax, Henry, if you're hard up," Staples said.

"No, it's not the money," Thoreau told him. "It's the principle of the thing."

Staples was troubled. "What do you think I should do, Henry?" he asked.

"Resign your job" was the prompt reply.

But Staples didn't want to do that and said so. Then he added, "Henry, if you don't pay, I'll have to lock you up pretty soon."

"As well now as any other time."

Staples immediately said, "Well, come along then." And he led Thoreau toward the town jail.

The Concord jail served as a place of imprisonment for all of Middlesex County, so it was a large and formidable building made of solid granite with walls two or three feet thick and with a ten-foot-high brick wall encircling its outer yard. It was in the center of town, backing up on the pond behind the Mill Dam. There were 18 narrow cells arranged in tiers three stories high. Each cell could hold several prisoners.

Staples unlocked the massive gate and led Thoreau into the prison yard, carefully shutting and locking the gate behind him.

Thoreau saw the other prisoners standing around in their shirt sleeves talking to each other. The jailer said, "Come, boys, it's time to lock up."

They obeyed peacefully enough and went into the jail. Staples introduced Thoreau to the prisoner whose cell he was to share and said that he was "a first-rate fellow and a clever man."

Once in the cell, this man showed Thoreau how things were managed in the jail. He wanted to know all about the newcomer and why he was there. Then Thoreau, in turn, learned about him.

"They accuse me of burning a barn," he said. "But I didn't do it."

On further questioning, Thoreau found out that he had been drunk, had gone to bed in someone's barn, had been smoking his pipe there, and thus may have started the fire. He had already been in jail for three months, but was not unhappy about it because he got his board for nothing and was well treated. Oddly enough he was allowed to go out each day to work in the fields without supervision.

He sat at one of the two windows in the cell telling Thoreau how prisoners had broken out and showed him where a grate had been sawed through. He also pointed out some of the verses prisoners had written on the white-washed walls.

Thoreau had trouble going to sleep because one of the prisoners in a lower cell kept saying, "What is life?" Finally Thoreau called out to him, "Well, what *is* life?" This silenced him, and the prisoners settled down to rest.

But Thoreau was still awake. He heard the town clock strike hour after hour, although he had never noticed it before. He could also hear the voices of the servants in the kitchen of the Middlesex Hotel, which was next door to the jail. He felt that he was getting a closer view of his native town, for he had never seen its institutions at work before. The jail was an arm of the Government, one of the ways in which a citizen could be compelled to fall in line with official policy.

And as he lay there, thoughts for an article to express what he felt were taking shape in his mind. He was willing to submit to the authority of government, but he believed that government first had to have the sanction and consent of the governed. The State had to recognize the individual as the power from which its authority came and treat him accordingly. Perhaps there would be such a State someday, perhaps it would even permit a few of its citizens "to live aloof from it, not meddling with it, nor embraced by it, who fulfilled all the duties of neighbors and fellow-men."

Somewhere, while following this line of thinking, Thoreau finally fell asleep. When he woke up, it was morning, and the jail was stirring to life.

Breakfast was served in the cell. Two small oblong tin pans—each with a pint of chocolate, some brown bread, and an iron spoon—were thrust through a hole in the door. When Thoreau's companion saw that he had not eaten all the bread, he took what was left, saying that it should be saved for lunch or dinner. Then he left the cell to help with the haying. He said good-bye and told Thoreau that he doubted whether he would ever see him again. He did not, but Thoreau was glad to learn that his cell companion was eventually found to be innocent. It was felt that his pipe had started the flames when he fell asleep in the barn, but that he had not set it on fire purposely. He was allowed to go free.

Soon after breakfast, Staples told Thoreau that some unknown person had appeared during the night to pay his tax, so there was no reason now to hold him. Thoreau did not want to go; he was there on principle, he said, and he intended to stay.

Staples refused to let him remain, saying, "Henry, if you won't go of your own accord, I'll have to put you out. You can't stay here."

Thoreau reluctantly agreed to leave. He was never able to find out who the mysterious—and doubtless well-meaning—person was who paid his tax. He thought that it might be Emerson or perhaps one of his aunts. Aunt Maria was likely to have done that sort of thing, but she would never admit doing it.

After he left the jail, Thoreau reclaimed his shoe at the cobbler's and joined one of the parties that were going on a huckleberry-picking expedition in the hills.

Thoreau's arrest was not forgotten. Everyone in town knew what had happened, and there was much talk, a good deal of it malicious. It was the custom in Concord to greet a released prisoner by looking at him through the crossed fingers of both hands, which were supposed to represent the grating of a jail window. No one dared to do that to Thoreau, but it was evident that many people disapproved of what he had done. Even Emerson criticized his action. A few days later, when he met Thoreau, he asked why he had chosen to go to jail.

"Why did you not?" was the calm reply. The words evidently had an effect, for Emerson wrote in his *Journal* that what Thoreau had done was better than the uncertainty of Abolitionists who denounced the war with Mexico but continued to pay the tax that financed it.

When Thoreau returned to his cabin at Walden Pond, he continued to live there as usual, writing in the mornings and then going out for long walks during the afternoons. Sometimes he would row his boat away from shore and let it drift as evening came on. When he played his flute, and the soft music trilled out over the quiet water, fish would gather around the boat and swim along with it as it drifted. At such times Thoreau would think about subjects for writing. Even if no one wanted to print his work, he could still continue to put down on paper what he wanted to say. In his *Journal* he wrote: "It is for want of original thought that one man's style is like anothers."

He kept working on *A Week* and continued to add to the manuscript that would someday be *Walden*.

At the end of August 1846 Thoreau went on a second trip to Maine. Again he visited his cousin and traveled with him into the interior. Wherever Thoreau went, he was interested in finding out all he could about the Indians. During his lifetime he gathered an amazing amount of information about them which has never been published.

They went by horse and buggy as far as they could, and when they reached a place where there were no roads, they had to travel on foot and then by boat. They were on their way to Mount Katahdin. It was Thoreau's ambition to climb that 5268-foot-high mountain, but on the ascent the others in his party got discouraged, so he had to go on alone. When he reached the cloud-covered summit it was so desolate that he saw Nature in a new aspect. He said that the windswept rocks "reminded me of the creations of the old epic and dramatic poets. . . . It was vast, Titanic, and such as man never inhabits." He did not like what he saw; this was a part of Nature that was so different from the pleasant countryside around

Concord that it frightened him. He was glad to rejoin his companions and descend to lower and less hostile levels.

People in Concord were curious about a well-educated young man who would leave his father's comfortable house and go off to the woods to live by himself. They wanted to know what Thoreau had to eat there. Was he ever lonesome? Or afraid? How much did he donate to charity? How many poor children did he maintain? One farmer, while driving an ox team, asked how Thoreau could get along only on vegetables, quite forgetting that his huge and powerful animals ate nothing else. Most of the questions the townspeople asked were just as silly, but Thoreau sensed that behind them was an underlying dissatisfaction with the lives they led. They might scoff at him, but their own existence evidently lacked something even if they did not know quite what it was.

In order to satisfy his townspeople's curiosity—and perhaps persuade them that there was more to life than grubbing for money—he gave two lectures in February 1847 about his experiences at Walden Pond. He told his audience that he did not "mean to prescribe rules to strong and valiant natures" or to "speak to those who are well employed . . . and they know whether they are well employed or not." He wanted to appeal "mainly to the mass of men who are discontented, and idly complaining of the hardness of their lot or of the times, when they might improve them. . . . I also have in my mind that seemingly wealthy, but most terribly impoverished class of all, who have accumulated dross, but know not how to use it, or get rid of it, and thus have forged their own golden or silver fetters."

In *Walden* Thoreau stated why he went to the woods:

I wished to live deliberately, to front only the essential facts of life, and to see if I could not learn what it had to teach, and not, when I came to die, discover that I had not lived. . . . I wanted to live deeply and suck out all the marrow of life, to live so sturdily and Spartan-like as to put to rout all that was not life, to cut a broad swath and shave close, to drive life into a corner, and reduce it to its lowest terms, and, if it proved to be mean, why then to get the whole and genuine meanness of it, and publish its meanness to the world; or if it were sublime, to know it by experience.

When he lectured at Concord, this was the first time he let the public know about the details of life in his woodland cabin. A year later he had more to say when he wrote a long letter to Horace Greeley which Greeley printed in the New York *Tribune.* Then the world learned that Thoreau had supported himself for five years by the labor of his own hands and that he had spent two years and two months in a house he had built himself— and all this at an expense of only 27 cents a week.

Walden, the book, had been under way for some time, but it was to be some years before the reading public would see it. Meanwhile, Thoreau kept on with the revisions of *A Week* and continued to look for a publisher. Both books had been started in the Walden Pond cabin, but neither was to be finished there.

During the winter of 1846–1847, a hundred Irish workmen came to the pond to cut ice. The railroad brought them from Cambridge every day and took them back at night. Big, oblong blocks of ice were dragged by horses to the shore where they were heaped up in a huge pile that "looked like a vast blue fort" estimated to contain about 10,000 tons of ice.

For sixteen days the pond was crowded with busy men whose voices resounded in the still winter air. Then they were gone, and the great ice palace "became covered with rime and icicles [until] it looked like a venerable moss-grown and hoary ruin, built of azure-tinted marble, the abode of Winter."

Thoreau liked to think that the ice would be taken by ship to warm parts of the world and that people in Charleston, New Orleans, Madras, Bombay, and Calcutta would drink the water from Walden Pond. But this did not happen, for something went wrong with the market for ice, and only a small part of the pile was taken away. The rest, covered with hay and boards, stood on the western shore of the pond through the following summer and the next, and did not finally melt away until September 1848. "Thus the pond recovered the greater part," Thoreau said.

Places where the workmen had cut holes in the ice quickly refroze, and the pond was soon covered again with a thick sheet of ice. But the winter was ending, and spring sunshine slowly turned the great white sheet to water.

With the return of spring, Thoreau again tried to get *A Week* published, but without success. He did not neglect his *Journal*, but kept adding to it and also clipping out passages to use in the manuscripts he was writing. His *Journal* was so valuable a source that when

Emerson wanted him to contribute to a transatlantic magazine he was hoping to start, Thoreau told him, "I am more interested in the private journal than the public one."

In 1847, which was the tenth anniversary of Thoreau's graduation from Harvard, the class secretary sent him a questionnaire. When he finally answered it, he said he had almost forgotten that he had ever been in college. As for his occupation, he was "a schoolmaster—a private Tutor, a Surveyor—a Gardener, a Farmer—a Painter, I mean a House Painter, a Carpenter, a Mason, a Day-Laborer, a Pencil-Maker, a Glass-paper Maker, a Writer, and sometimes a Poetaster."

Pleasant as life had been in the cabin at Walden Pond, Thoreau was ready to leave. Emerson was going on a long lecture tour in Europe, starting in October. He invited his friend to take care of his household again. On September 6, 1847, just two years, two months, and two days after Thoreau had first occupied the cabin, he moved out for good. In his book about it he said, "I left the woods for as good a reason as I went there. Perhaps it seemed to me that I had several more lives to live, and could not spare any more time for that one."

If that seems vague, Thoreau was uncertain about the reason, even to himself. In his *Journal*, nearly five years later, he wrote:

But why I changed? Why I left the woods? I do not think I can tell. I have often wished myself back. I do not know any better how I came to go there. Perhaps it is none of my business, even if it is yours. Perhaps I wanted a change. There was a little stagnation, it may be. About 2 o'clock in the afternoon the world's axle creaked as if it needed greasing. . . . Perhaps if I lived there much longer, I might live there forever. One would think twice before he accepted heaven on such terms.

Emerson bought the cabin because it was on his land. His Irish gardener acquired it but never used it. Finally it was hauled away to a farm north of Concord where it was made into a storehouse and at last fell into decay.

During the time it remained in the Walden woods Thoreau must often have visited it. Perhaps memories of those two happy years returned to him when he saw the little building again. His stay there was the only time he ever had a home of his own.

During the summer of 1848, Emerson commissioned Bronson Alcott to build a summerhouse. Alcott and his family needed money, and Emerson was always ready to help friends in need. Emerson, Alcott, and Thoreau went to the Walden Pond woodlot to cut tree posts for the house, but Emerson quickly proved to be so clumsy with an axe that he gave up the unaccustomed work and went home. Alcott was not much better. When he cut down a tree it began to fall in such a way that its branches were about to become entangled in those of another tree, and Thoreau had to use all his strength to push its trunk away so it would land in a better position After that he did most of the work himself.

Alcott, however, was the architect. His plans made

the garden house into an elaborate, overornamented structure which Channing called a "pancake" with "a wickerwork skull; then a head of moss . . . lastly, a straw night-cap." There were few straight lines in it; almost everything was curved and curlicued. Alcott never took a plain piece of wood if he could get a gnarled and twisted branch which he admired for its grotesque beauty.

As a result, the strange-looking summerhouse was seldom used. Thoreau finally planted some pine trees around it to hide the ugly structure from sight.

WITH THE
EMERSONS AGAIN

1847

No word is oftener on the lips of men than Friendship, and indeed no thought is more familiar to their aspirations. All men are dreaming of it, and its drama, which is always a tragedy, is enacted daily.

On October 5, 1847, Thoreau, Lidian, and the Alcotts went to Boston to see Emerson leave for Europe. The ship he was going on, appropriately named the *Washington Irving* for another American writer, was a small sailing vessel with exceedingly cramped quarters for its passengers. Thoreau noted that Emerson's stateroom was "a carpeted dark closet, about six feet square, with a large keyhole for a window." And this was for a winter voyage, during which the little ship would be tossed about on the rough seas. He did not envy Emerson. Europe was far away, and it was surely better to read about it than to go there in such a miserable cabin. Thoreau did not mind confined living space, but he wanted plenty of room when he got outdoors. The ship's deck was no place to walk. A few steps would cover it; then you had to pace back and forth like a caged animal.

He was glad to get back to Concord where he immediately began to prepare the Emerson house for the coming of winter. It was pleasant being there with Lidian and the three children. When he wrote to Emerson in England, he said, "Lidian and I make very good housekeepers. She is a very dear sister to me. Ellen and Edith and Eddy and Aunty Brown [Lidian's sister] keep up the tragedy and comedy and tragic-comedy of life as usual. . . . Eddy . . . very seriously asked me the other day, 'Mr. Thoreau, will you be my father? . . .' So you must come back soon or you will be superseded."

He also told Emerson that a Miss Sophia Ford, who was fifteen years older than he, wanted to marry him. She had been a teacher in Concord and had kept school in Emerson's renovated barn. Thoreau was amused, but he had declined her offer and told Emerson that he "had really anticipated no such foe as this." There was gossip in Concord that still another spinster had set her cap for Thoreau. But he was determined to remain a bachelor and did so.

During this time he continued his efforts to get a publisher for *A Week*, but still could not find one. Four companies had already turned down the manuscript.

Early in January he lectured at the Concord Lyceum about the Maine woods and then made the material into a series of articles for Greeley to place. He also wrote an essay on "Friendship," which no magazine would take, so he put it into the manuscript of *A Week*. He gave another lecture at the Lyceum later in the month.

This time he spoke about his night in jail and what it meant. His famous "Civil Disobedience" came from the lecture.

The war with Mexico was ending and was finally terminated on February 2, 1848, by the Treaty of Guadalupe Hidalgo. No one in the eastern part of the United States or in Mexico yet knew it, but gold had been discovered at Sutter's Mill in California a few days before the treaty was signed. Among other things, the treaty ceded California to the United States. California was to be enormously valuable—and not only because of its gold.

Ordinarily Thoreau began his letters to Emerson with "Dear Friend" or "My Dear Friend," but on February 23, he wrote "Dear Waldo," and then went on to say: "For I think I have heard that that is your name. . . . Whatever I may call you, I know you better than I know your name." Emerson always addressed Thoreau as "Henry." His reply to the "Dear Waldo" letter was cordial enough, but Thoreau thereafter went back to addressing him as "Dear Friend." Perhaps Thoreau's letter marked the height of the complex relationship between the two men.

The February 23 letter carried bad news. It said that Lidian was ill, so ill that she had been in bed for weeks, had constant nausea, and was yellow with jaundice. One might expect that such news would bring Emerson back from Europe in a hurry, but it did not. Word traveled so slowly in those days that people tended to discount it. By the time Emerson received word about his wife he may have thought that she was well on her way to recovery. At any rate he had gone on to Scotland and then went from there to Paris, where the French Revolution of 1848 was brewing. He did not sail home until the end of July.

While Emerson was in Europe, Thoreau received a letter from Harrison Gray Otis Blake, whom he had known at Harvard, where the somewhat older man had then been attending the Divinity School. Blake had been ordained as a minister, but had changed his career to become a schoolteacher in Worcester, Massachusetts. He had just reread "Aulus Persius Flaccus," a minor essay on the Roman poet which Thoreau had written for *The Dial* in 1840. He was now so moved by it that he wanted to express his admiration. He had been particularly struck by a remark Thoreau had made to him in Concord when he said that he wished to retire from civilization and that he would not miss the society of his friends. Blake also had thought of doing this. "But, alas!" he said, "I shiver on the brink."

Thoreau replied to him at length, and thus began the most important correspondence of his life. In his first letter he said: "I do believe in simplicity. It is astonishing, as well as sad, how many trivial affairs even the wisest man thinks he must attend to in a day. . . . When the mathematician would solve a difficult problem, he first frees the equation of all incumbrances and reduces it to its simplest terms. So simplify the problem of life, distinguish the necessary and the real. Probe the earth to see where your main roots run."

And then he went on to say: "I have no designs on society—or nature—or God. I am simply what I am. . . . I know that the enterprise is worthy—I know that things work well. I have heard no bad news."

In another letter he added: "I am too easily contented with a slight and almost animal happiness. My happiness is a good deal like that of the woodchucks."

During the spring of 1848 Thoreau received several payments for articles that Horace Greeley had placed or bought. It was the first time he ever got an appreciable sum of money for his writing. It was only $100, but Thoreau called it a "sudden accession of wealth." He also told Greeley something about the way he had lived at Walden. Greeley was so much impressed that he printed that part of Thoreau's letter in the *Tribune*, where some of America's most influential people would see it.

Greeley urged Thoreau to concentrate on articles for magazines because publication there would let people know who he was. "Ten years hence will do for publishing books," he wrote. And he also suggested that Thoreau make his pieces shorter. They tended to be too long to fit into the closely crowded pages of popular magazines.

When Emerson returned from England, Thoreau moved to his father's Texas House. During the fall he earned a little money by doing odd jobs and working for a while in the pencil factory. He also began to turn his attention to surveying. Anyone could do manual work, but measuring and mapping land requires a knowledge of mathematics and a certain amount of skill in using precision instruments. He had a poster printed to advertise his services, and the next year bought a notebook for his surveying records.

In the autumn of 1848, Thoreau achieved a certain small measure of fame although it was not to his liking. James Russell Lowell, who was rapidly becoming well known as a writer, satirized his fellow authors in his *Fable for Critics*. In this long poem he devoted a good deal of space to Emerson and then went on to say:

There comes ———, for instance; to see him's rare sport,
Tread in Emerson's tracks with legs painfully short;
How he jumps, how he strains, and gets red in the face,
To keep up with the mystagogue's natural pace!
He follows as close as a stick to a rocket,
His fingers exploring the prophet's each pocket.
Fie, for shame brother bard; with good fruit of your own,
Can't you let Neighbor Emerson's orchards alone?

It was bad enough to be caricaturized for his appearance but to be accused of pilfering Emerson's ideas was intolerable. However, there was nothing Thoreau could do. He had to restrain his anger and keep silent. But he never forgot Lowell's unkind jests.

All his various activities, plus lectures, earned Thoreau a slender but adequate income. Hawthorne, who had moved to Salem, came to his help by obtaining a lecture for him there. He spoke on "Student Life in New England, Its Economy." What he said was used in the first chapter of *Walden*.

On the way back from Salem he went with Hawthorne to have dinner with Henry Wadsworth Longfellow at his beautiful Revolutionary-period house in Cambridge. Longfellow, whose *Evangeline* had recently been published, was becoming one of the most successful poets in America. Ellery Channing was also present. It would be interesting to know what the four writers talked about, but unfortunately no record of their conversation was made.

The lecture at Salem brought Thoreau an invitation to speak at Gloucester on December 20. The serious nature of what he had to say about the faults of society antagonized the newspaper reporter who had been sent to cover the lecture, and he gave it a bad notice.

In a letter to his cousin George Thatcher in Maine, Thoreau paraphrased Barnum when he said: "Whatever they may say is not to the purpose only as it serves as an advertisement of me."

LECTURER, WRITER, PROTESTER ...

1847-1849

To affect the quality of the day, that is the highest of the arts. Every man is tasked to make his life, even in its details, worthy of the contemplation of his most elevated and critical hour.

The people who attended lectures at the Concord Lyceum got another installment of the *Walden* story early in January 1849 when Thoreau spoke on "White Beans and Walden Pond." He gave two lectures in Salem in February, one in Portland, Maine, in March, and three in Worcester in April. Since these were all based on early chapters of *Walden*, it is evident that he was then working on the manuscript.

But he still wanted to get *A Week on the Concord and Merrimack Rivers* published. He wrote to Ticknor and Company in Boston suggesting that they issue the book and told them that *Walden* would also soon be completed. In their reply they said that they did not want *A Week* but would take *Walden*. Then they offered to do *A Week* first but at the author's expense.

A cash payment of $450 was required. Since this was more money than Thoreau had—or was able to raise— the deal naturally fell through.

He then went back to James Munroe and Company, one of the houses that had already seen the manuscript, and was able to persuade them to take it but on miserable terms. They would pay for the printing and binding and then deduct these costs from the money realized from sales. Thoreau, however, had to guarantee them that they would eventually be paid in full. It was an expensive arrangement, for the sales of *A Week* turned out to be negligible. But, like most authors, Thoreau was eager to see his work in print, and he agreed to the proposal. The manuscript went to the printer who began to send proofs in the middle of March. For the rest of that month and for all of April, Thoreau was busy reading them. It was a lot of work, for the typesetting was so bad that there were more than a thousand errors. And in one place a whole passage had been left out.

The book was published on May 30. A few days before that, Thoreau traveled to Boston to see the finished copies. Only 1,000 had been printed, of which 450 were bound, while the others were held in sheets that could be bound later if there was enough demand for them.

In the back of the book was an advertisement that read: "Will soon be published, *Walden*, or *Life in the Woods*. By Henry D. Thoreau." But it was to be five years before *Walden* was issued.

A Week on the Concord and Merrimack Rivers has an introduction that describes the Concord River; then there are seven chapters, each one named after a day of the week, with Saturday as the first.

In the Friday chapter Thoreau had a great deal to say about poetry. There he wrote:

> The poet is no tender slip of fairy stock . . . but the toughest son of earth and of Heaven, and by his greater strength and endurance, his fainting companions will recognize the God in him. It is the worshippers of beauty, after all, who have done the real pioneer work of the world.

And in this chapter he summed up the essence of what he thought of himself when he said:

> My life has been the poem I would have writ,
> But I could not both live and utter it.

Yet, for all his praise of poetry, he also said, "Great prose, of equal elevation, commands our respect more than great verse, since it implies a more permanent and level height, a life more pervaded with the grandeur of the thought."

The publication of *A Week* attracted a fair amount of attention. Nearly a hundred copies were sent to noted people in America and England in the hope that it would impress them enough to write something favorable about it. Except for some of Thoreau's friends, few of them did. The reviews that appeared during the summer were generally good, but they failed to send readers into the bookstores.

By autumn it was obvious that the book was a financial failure and that its author was going to have to pay his publisher a considerable sum of money. He went to work again in the pencil factory, but it was a bad time for selling pencils, and he had to dispose of many of them at a loss. Munroe and Company had to wait four years for their money, but they eventually got it. All that Thoreau got was the right to say that he was the author of a book that very few people had even heard of and that even fewer had read.

Under the circumstances, Munroe and Company had no interest in bringing out *Walden*, even though they had advertised that it would "soon be published." Thoreau, however, did not put his manuscript away. He kept working at it and was to continue to do so for several more years.

Before *A Week* was issued, Thoreau had what was to be a bit of good fortune although there was no reason for him to think of it as such, for it did not come to fruition until long after he was dead. Elizabeth Peabody, who had a bookstore in Boston, wrote for permission to print the text of his lecture about the night he had spent in jail for not paying his taxes. It was to appear in her new magazine, *Aesthetic Papers*, which she hoped would replace *The Dial*. The first number came out on May 14, 1849. It had contributions from Emerson and Hawthorne as well as Thoreau, but it never went beyond its one and only first issue. In it, Thoreau's lecture, which he had called "The Rights and Duties of the Individual in Relation to Government," was now entitled "Resistance to Civil Government." It did not get its final title, "Civil Disobedience," until it was printed in the book *A Yankee in Canada* after Thoreau's death.

The essay in *Aesthetic Papers* was ignored and quickly disappeared from public attention along with Miss Peabody's ill-fated venture in magazine publishing. Its time had not yet come and was not to do so until the twentieth century when men like Tolstoy, Gandhi, and Martin Luther King, Jr., would realize its importance and bring it back into circulation for a new audience.

Yet this long-neglected essay expressed Thoreau's most advanced and original thought on the individual's relationship to a government whose actions he could not condone. The United States in the late 1840's seemed to be in danger of being dominated by the proslavery South. The outcome of the war with Mexico had given the slaveholders more power, and they were reaching out for additional territory in Kansas and Nebraska. Now that the Treaty of Guadalupe Hidalgo, which settled the war with Mexico, had ceded California and New Mexico to the United States, there was also going to be a struggle over establishing slavery in the recently acquired Far Western territories. Both Florida and Texas had entered the Union in 1845 as slave states. Proslavery forces seemed to be taking over the country.

The war with Mexico had not quite ended when Thoreau delivered his lecture at the Concord Lyceum, yet everything he said then was still valid. He made a few additions for *Aesthetic Papers*—mostly quotations from Daniel Webster, who had not yet fallen from favor with antislavery people, as he was to do when he supported the Compromise of 1850 with its Fugitive Slave Law.

The now famous "Civil Disobedience" essay said that there was a higher law than the ones written in the books; that this law was man's conscience, his knowledge of right and wrong. When the written laws, like those supporting slavery, were unquestionably evil, it was time for the higher law to take over. Then people would be justified in breaking the established laws, but those who did so must be willing to pay the penalty for what they were doing, even if it meant being put in jail. From jail, the protester could speak out to denounce the law he was breaking and so win others over to his side.

The majority have power, he said,

because they are physically the strongest. . . . How does it become a man to behave toward this American government to-day? I answer, that he cannot without disgrace be associated with it. I cannot for an instant recognize that political organization as *my* government which is the *slave's* government also. . . . Unjust laws exist: shall we be content to obey them, or shall we endeavor to amend them, and obey them until we have succeeded, or shall we transgress them at once? . . . I do not hesitate to say that those who call themselves Abolitionists should at once effectually withdraw their support, both in person and property, from the government . . . and not wait till they constitute a majority of one, before they suffer the right to prevail through them. I think that it is enough if they have God on their side, without waiting for that other one. Moreover, any man more right than his neighbors constitutes a majority of one already.

Thoreau did not attempt to define what "right" was. According to Transcendentalist belief, man was born with the ability to determine the difference between right and wrong, and only the evil nature of society made him lose that innate ability. But what mortal could decide which was the God-given "right" and which the man-engendered wrong?

Thoreau explained his own attitude toward the problem:

I have never declined paying the highway tax, because I am as desirous of being a good neighbor as I am of being a bad subject; and, as for supporting schools, I am doing my part to educate my fellow-countrymen now. It is for no particular item in the tax bill that I refuse to pay it. I simply wish to refuse allegiance to the State, to withdraw and stand aloof from it effectually. I do not care to trace the course of my dollar, if I could, till it buys a man or a musket to shoot one with.

On June 14, 1849, only a few weeks after Thoreau's first two important publications appeared, his sister Helen, who had been ailing for some time with tuberculosis, died at the age of thirty-six.

At the funeral her brother sat silent throughout the services. Then he got up, took a music box, wound it up, and turned it on. From it came a plaintive melody that was "like no earthly tune."

The Thoreaus' pencil-making business was changing its product and becoming more profitable as a result. Electrotypes, which were replacing stereotypes as printing plates, required finely powdered graphite to conduct current when copper was deposited electrically to re-

produce the type. A Boston company gave the Thoreaus
big orders for graphite but made them promise not to
tell what the material was to be used for, because the
process was still a secret one. They were to continue to
make pencils, but only to cover up the better-paying
sale of graphite.

Emerson's son recalls what happened at this time:

Henry had to oversee the mill [which was attached to the
Texas House], bring the lead down, and help at the heavier
part of boxing and packing. . . . The impalpable powder so
pervaded the house . . . that a friend . . . found the [piano]
keys coated with it. Thoreau . . . would probably much
earlier have succumbed to a disease, hereditary in his family,
had he held more closely to his trade with its irritant dust.
The part he was obliged to bear in it certainly rendered
him more susceptible to pulmonary disease.

In September 1849, perhaps encouraged by the more
profitable nature of his business, Thoreau's father bought
a new home on Main Street near the center of Concord.
Although it was much larger and finer than the Texas
House, extensive renovations were made to improve it.
The barn, joined to the main building, was to be the
graphite factory. The entire structure was painted yellow and thus was known as the Yellow House. It still
stands, although it is now painted white.

There was so much work to be done that the Thoreaus were not able to move into their new residence
until eleven months after they bought it. Then the
thirty-three-year-old writer, lecturer, naturalist, and
pencil maker had new and far more spacious quarters for

himself. He occupied a finished attic, which he lined
with shelves for his books and storage boxes for his
collections of botanical and mineral specimens. Here,
too, were his Indian relics and other odds and ends that
interested him. The room was furnished with the few
sparse pieces he had used in his Walden cabin—the cot,
the desk, and the chairs. It was quiet up there, far removed from the hustle and bustle of the boardinghouse
downstairs. The only disadvantage was that the room
under the roof could get terribly hot in the summer.
Winter was no problem; a wood stove kept the place
warm then.

These upstairs living quarters were to be Thoreau's
last home. Over the remaining years, the collections
grew larger, and volume after volume was added to the
Journal. Sometime toward the end of his life, he made a
box out of river boards to contain the 39 notebooks that
are the record of his life and thoughts. The multi-
volumed *Journal* is now one of the treasures of the Pier-
pont Morgan Library in New York.

Thoreau, who was a great reader, never had enough
money to buy the books he wanted. Nor were they always available in Concord, even in Emerson's well-
stocked private library. But the Harvard Library in
Cambridge had practically everything that Thoreau ever
needed. The only trouble was that he was not a member
of the faculty nor did he live within ten miles of Cambridge. Therefore, according to the rules, he was not
entitled to borrow books. He had encountered this dif-
ficulty in 1841 and had then won the right to take out

books. But he had allowed the privilege to lapse, and now that he was becoming more and more interested in Oriental literature, he again needed to use the library. On September 17, 1849, he addressed a letter to the president of Harvard:

I wish to get permission to take books from the College library. . . . I . . . ask this, not merely because I am an alumnus of Harvard . . . but *because I have chosen letters for my profession.* . . . Though books are to some extent my stock and tools, I have not the usual means with which to purchase them. I therefore regard myself as one whom especially the library was created to serve. . . . I ask only that the University may help to finish the education, whose foundation she helped to lay.

The president granted permission but wrote on the letter "One Year." Thoreau, however, paid no attention to the limitation and continued to use the Harvard Library as long as he lived.

...TRAVELER, SURVEYOR, AND NATURALIST

1849-1853

The really efficient laborer will be found not to crowd his day with work, but will saunter to his task surrounded by a wide halo of ease and leisure. . . . He is only earnest to secure the kernels of time, and does not exaggerate the value of the husk.

It was rather late in 1849—in October—when Thoreau and Ellery Channing decided to visit Cape Cod. At Boston they found the weather so bad that the steamer had not yet arrived from Provincetown. When they heard that there had been a disastrous shipwreck at nearby Cohasset, they went there to see what had happened. Ellen Sewall, now Mrs. Joseph Osgood, with whom Thoreau had once been in love, was living there. They visited her, and her husband accompanied them to the shore to view the wreck.

It was a terrible sight. The brig *St. John* from Ireland had run on the rocks near the shore and had broken up under the force of the pounding sea. It was believed that 145 immigrants had been drowned. The beach was covered with bodies, and the waves were bringing in more. Coffins and rough boxes, which had been brought to the scene, were rapidly being filled up, but it was evident that there would not be enough of them.

Thoreau was a good psychologist when he said, "It was not so impressive a scene as I might have expected. If I had found one body cast upon the beach in some lonely place, it would have affected me more."

He also noted that "in the very midst of the crowd . . . there were men with carts busily collecting the seaweed which the storm cast up. . . . though they were often obliged to separate fragments of clothing from it, and they might at any moment have found a human body under it. Drown who might, they did not forget that this weed was a valuable manure."

After this inauspicious beginning to their journey, Thoreau and Channing went on to Sandwich, where they boarded a stagecoach in the rain that poured down the next morning. They reached Orleans and stayed overnight there to be greeted by more rain when they awoke. That day they traveled on foot and slept in a Wellfleet oysterman's house. Its elderly owner told them a great deal about the Cape's fresh-water ponds, about his memories of the Revolution, and about the ships that had been wrecked along that treacherous coast.

They spent the next night at Highland Light and then stayed in Provincetown for two days. They explored the sea beaches beyond the town and were impressed by the huge waves that were breaking on the shore.

Then they took the noon steamer to Boston and were

back in Concord before night came. In that one day they had come from the seaside fishing village of Provincetown, with its bare, sparse landscape dominated by sand dunes and fish-drying racks, to the bright colors of the autumn foliage in Concord. In Concord the houses were big and comfortable, almost luxurious compared to the unpainted shacks they had seen on the Cape. Massachusetts suddenly seemed bigger. Certainly it was a varied state despite its small size.

Thoreau was so impressed by Cape Cod that he read everything he could find about the long sandy arm which sticks out into the ocean. During the winter he gave three lectures on the Cape and kept gathering material for a series of magazine articles.

Because of his continuing interest he went back alone to Provincetown in June 1850 and walked from there as far as Chatham where he turned back to Provincetown. On the way he revisited Highland Light and talked again with the old Wellfleet oysterman. He stayed only for a few days, but during that brief time he was able to get the information he needed and also explore the seacoast near Eastham and Chatham.

During that same year he got a good compass and took up surveying seriously. He completed more than twenty surveys in 1850 and as a result became even better known as an expert in plotting property boundaries and making careful maps of them. The work had the great advantage of keeping him out in the open and also of taking him into territory he would otherwise not have seen. Through it he sometimes met interesting people, particularly old ones who would tell him about

Concord as it had been when they were young. Unfortunately, however, he often had to deal with money-grubbing farmers and selectmen whom he despised.

Margaret Fuller, who had edited *The Dial* and made a name for herself by her writings, had gone to Italy where she married Count Ossoli and bore him a son. In July word came to Concord that a ship had been wrecked off the shore of Fire Island near New York. And on it were the Ossolis. It was believed that they had been lost and that with them went the manuscript Margaret Fuller had been writing on the Revolution of 1848 in Italy.

Emerson asked Thoreau to go to Fire Island to see what could be found. He arrived there five days after the wreck. By that time nearly everything of any value that had come ashore had been taken away. When he wrote to Emerson, he said that a "broken desk in a bag—containing no very valuable papers—a large black leather trunk—with an upper and under apartment [*sic*] —the upper holding books & papers—a carpet bag probably Ossolis and one of his? shoes—are all the Ossolis' effects known to have been found."

He did come across the Count's coat and ripped a button off it to take back to Concord. In his *Journal* he said of it: "Held up, it intercepts the light and casts a shadow—an *actual* button—yet all the life it is connected with is less substantial to me, and interests me less, than my faintest dreams. . . . Our thoughts are the epochs of our life: all else is but as a journal of the winds that blew while we were here."

In the autumn of 1850 a round-trip excursion from
Boston to Montreal for only seven dollars was advertised
by the railroad. Thoreau and Ellery Channing bought
tickets and went by train through New Hampshire,
Vermont, and New York. It was a long journey, part
of which was made on a steamer that took them up
Lake Champlain. Then they had to go by train to
Canada. In Montreal, Thoreau saw great numbers of
priests and soldiers for the first time.

They went by steamer down the St. Lawrence River
to Quebec. There they walked to Montmorency Falls.
Thoreau was not dressed for Canadian weather. As
night came on he felt chilled and began to show signs of
catching a cold.

The total cost of the trip to Canada was only $12.75,
but it had not been a very happy journey. "What I got
by going to Canada was a cold," Thoreau complained.
But he wanted to write some salable articles on what he
had seen, so he began to read about that country, just
as he had about Cape Cod. During the process of shaping up his material, he gave two lectures and then—
through Horace Greeley—placed them as a serial in
Putnam's Monthly.

After three installments had appeared, Thoreau objected to the editor's omission of some critical remarks
he had made about the priesthood. He asked for the
manuscript to be returned, and publication in the magazine ceased.

Lectures about Canada proved to be less popular than
those about Cape Cod, Walden, and other familiar

American scenes. But Thoreau was busier than usual
with lecture dates during the winter of 1850–1851. And
his lectures often supplied material for publishable
articles, even though some of them were not to appear
in print until many years later.

The census of 1850 showed that the United States
had a population of 23,191,876, of whom 3,204,314
were slaves. And the Compromise of 1850, in an effort
to hold the dividing nation together, gave the slaveholders the right to pursue runaways into the Northern
states and forcibly take them back into bondage. This
Fugitive Slave Act outraged the Abolitionists more than
anything the Federal government had yet done.

In February 1851, Boston had a dramatic example of
what the new law meant. A fugitive slave named Shad-
rach was captured and put into jail until he could be returned to the South. The Abolitionists, aided by many
free blacks, stormed the building and whisked him away
to Concord and from there to Canada and freedom.

The next captured fugitive was not so lucky. He was
Thomas Sims, who was arrested and jailed in Boston on
April 3. By this time the authorities had learned how to
deal with such captives. Sims was so heavily guarded
that an attempted rescue failed, and he was sent back to
Georgia.

There was no doubt that the Fugitive Slave Act was a
victory for the South. All that month Thoreau's *Journal*
was filled with angry reactions to it. "I hear a good deal
said about trampling this law under foot. Why, one
need not go out of his way to do that. This law lies not

at the level of the head or the reason. Its natural habitat is in the dirt. . . . He who walks with freedom . . . will inevitably tread on it."

Although he was not yet 34, Thoreau felt that he was growing old. In May he had good reason to. His teeth had been giving him trouble, and the dentists of the time had no way of treating them other than to pull them all out. When Thoreau was given ether for the painful operation, he found its heady effects delightful. "You go beyond the furthest star," he said.

He was pleased with the dentures which replaced his own teeth and told Emerson that if he had known how good they were he would have had the work done sooner.

During the summer Thoreau discovered the charm of taking night walks, especially when the moon was full and the sky was clear. He found out that one had to see the countryside by night as well as by day to get a complete notion of it. At such time, he said, he seemed "to be nearer the origin of things."

Concord people did not go out at night unless they had to, but walking in the daytime was popular, so much so that people occasionally wanted to accompany Thoreau. He nearly always avoided them. "I know of but one or two persons with whom I can afford to walk," he said. Ellery Channing was one. In his way he was as strange as Thoreau. Perhaps that was why they got along so well.

It was fortunate that Thoreau found Channing's com-

pany agreeable, for he was no longer so friendly with
Emerson as he had once been. Emerson was aware of
this and had made efforts to restore the relationship.
Thoreau, however, did not respond. Both men's journals
show how keenly they regretted the loss of what had
meant so much to them, but neither could understand
why their friendship was deteriorating nor think of any
way to restore it.

There is no doubt that Thoreau was distrustful, far
more so than Emerson. His *Journal* entries show this.
They do not mention Emerson by name, but the
"friend" so often referred to is almost surely he. "I
thought that we had not withdrawn very far asunder,"
he writes. "But now that my friend rashly, thought-
lessly, profanely speaks, *recognizing* the distance between us, that distance seems infinitely increased."

The break, which had already begun, was to widen,
yet the two men never became openly hostile to each
other. They continued to converse as if nothing had
happened.

During the summer of 1851 the first telegraph lines
were strung along the railroad route. When Thoreau
heard the wires humming in the wind, making an un-
earthly music, he was delighted. He commented on the
"telegraph harp" again and again in his *Journal*. There
was no doubt that he had a keen sense of appreciation
for good music, but he had been born into a time and
place where it was seldom heard.

Late in July he went on foot along the south shore of
Boston Harbor and again visited the Osgoods in Cohasset.

He also stopped at Marston and Mary Watson's arboretum in Plymouth to inspect its unusual trees. From Plymouth he walked back to Boston, where he spent some time in the Boston Society of Natural History.

In March 1852, Hawthorne bought the house in which the Alcotts had lived and which Louisa May Alcott was later to make famous in *Little Women*. Hawthorne had already made a name for himself by the recent publication of *The Scarlet Letter* and *The House of Seven Gables*. Other contemporaries of Thoreau were also on their way to fame. Herman Melville's *Moby-Dick* had come out during the previous year, and Harriet Beecher Stowe's *Uncle Tom's Cabin* was becoming one of America's first best sellers. Edgar Allan Poe's work, however, was finished. He had died in 1849 after a lifetime of poverty and rejection.

During the autumn of 1852, Thoreau evidently was hard at work making more revisions in the manuscript of *Walden,* for his *Journal* shows that he was visiting Walden Pond day after day.

The year 1851 had been an eventful one for Thoreau; 1852 and 1853 were not. He went quietly about his business of surveying, lecturing, and making observations about Nature. The rift in his friendship with Emerson was widening still further as a *Journal* entry for May 24 shows: "Talked, or tried to talk, with R.W.E. Lost my time—nay almost my identity. He, assuming a false opposition where there was no difference of opinion, talked to the wind—told me what I knew—and I lost my time trying to imagine myself somebody else to oppose him."

One thing, however, that Thoreau and Emerson stood firmly together on was their determined opposition to slavery. Moncure Conway, a Virginian who had become an Abolitionist, visited the Thoreaus when a fugitive slave had taken refuge in their house. Conway said that Thoreau "watched the singularly tender and lowly devotion of the scholar to the slave. He must be fed, his swollen feet bathed, and he must think of nothing but rest. . . . This coolest and calmest of men drew near the trembling Negro and bade him feel at home and have no fear."

Later that year a free Negro woman stayed with the Thoreaus while she tried to raise money to buy her husband from the Virginian who owned him. Thoreau was outraged when he learned that the owner wanted to make a $200 profit on the sale.

He also came to the aid of a poor Irish laborer who had won a prize of four dollars for his quickness at spading at the local agricultural fair. His employer, who was noted for his meanness, was trying to get the pathetically small prize away from the man who had earned it.

During the autumn of 1853, Thoreau again went on a trip through Maine with his cousin, George Thatcher of Bangor. They had an Indian guide who found a moose for Thatcher to shoot. Thoreau disapproved of the senseless killing, for they did not need meat or want the hide.

They went by canoe up the Penobscot River where Thoreau had a chance to study Indian life. Heavy rain

put an end to their journey, and they returned to
Bangor. From there Thoreau took a steamer to Boston
with a notebook full of observations to be worked into
lectures and articles.

The year 1853 ended badly for Thoreau. In October
he received a wagonload of books, bound and unbound,
from Munroe and Company. They were 706 unsold
copies of *A Week on the Concord and Merrimack
Rivers*. He wrote ruefully: "I now have a library of
nearly 900 volumes, over 700 of which I wrote myself.
. . . This is authorship; these are the work of my brain."

And, in accordance with his contract, Thoreau had
had to pay the publisher for the unsold copies. In his
own account of the transaction he said that he had paid
out of pocket $290 for the edition and had received a
total of about $15 for it. Yet he was able to confide to
his *Journal:* "Nevertheless . . . I take up my pen to-night
to record what thought or experience I may have had,
with as much satisfaction as ever. Indeed, I believe that
this result is more inspiring and better for me than if a
thousand had bought my wares. It affects my privacy
less and leaves me freer."

He could not always be so philosophic however. Just
before Christmas he wrote:

I have offered myself much more earnestly as a lecturer
than as a surveyor. Yet I do not get employment as a lecturer; was not invited to lecture once last winter and only
once (without pay) this winter. *But* I can get surveying
enough, which a hundred others in this country can do as

well as I, though it is not boasting much to say that a hundred others in New England cannot lecture as well as I on my themes. But they who do not make the highest demand on you shall rue it. . . . Woe be to any generation that lets any higher faculty in its midst go unemployed!

THE PUBLICATION
OF *WALDEN*

1854

In most books, the I, *or first person, is omitted; in this book it will be retained; that, in respect to egotism, is the main difference. We commonly do not remember that it is, after all, always the first person that is speaking. I should not talk so much about myself if there were anybody else whom I knew as well.*

One might think that being reminded daily of the failure of his first book would have discouraged Thoreau, but he was able to live in the same room with 706 unwanted copies of *A Week* and yet go on with the writing of *Walden*.

The winter of 1853–1854 finally saw the completion of that book. Some time in March, Thoreau put down the last words of a manuscript that had become increasingly more complex, more crossed out, and more written over than anything he had yet done—or was ever to do again. He had begun writing it while he lived in the cabin by the pond from 1845 to 1847; then he kept revising it until he had put down seven drafts of the manuscript. Some time late in 1853 or very early in 1854, he made a complete new copy of his work, the eighth version of it. He did so because he had found a publisher for the book—and a good one too, Ticknor and Fields, as Ticknor and Company was now called. Noted authors like Hawthorne, Holmes, Longfellow, Lowell, and Whittier were on their list.

After his unhappy experience with Munroe and Company when they issued *A Week on the Concord and Merrimack Rivers* in 1849, Thoreau was fortunate in having found a firm like Ticknor and Fields to bring out *Walden*. They gave him a good royalty contract, agreed to print 2,000 copies and to sell the book for a dollar a copy.

Thoreau thought that he had made a "fair copy" of the manuscript for typesetting. Actually it was difficult to read as the printer's remarks on the proofs show.

But setting type for *Walden* went fast because a set of proofs had to be ready before June 7 when Fields was going to England. He hoped in this way to find a publisher there for the book and thus establish British copyright.

Thoreau got the first proofs of *Walden* on March 28. They were much better than the ones Munroe had sent him for *A Week*, but they needed careful reading as all proofs do. During the process he noted in his *Journal*: "In criticising your writing, trust your fine instinct. There are many things which we come very near questioning, but do not question. When I have sent off my manuscripts to the printer, certain objectionable sentences or expressions are sure to obtrude themselves on my attention with force, though I had not consciously suspected them before. My critical instinct then at once breaks the ice and comes to the surface."

And then, a few days later: "I find that I can criticise my composition best when I stand at a little distance from it,—when I do not see it, for instance. I make a little chapter of contents which enables me to recall it page by page to my mind, and judge it more impartially when the manuscript is out of the way."

That Thoreau should have been able to do this with the *Walden* manuscript is truly remarkable, for the pages that make up the first seven versions are a hodge-podge. The eighth version, the "fair copy" from which the type was set, has somehow disappeared. But Thoreau could not have been very familiar with it, since he saw it only for the short time between putting it on paper and sending it to the printer. He had lived with the various other versions for so long, however, that he must have known much of the wording by heart. Yet he was never satisfied with the order and arrangement of the text; he was forever changing the position of sentences, paragraphs, pages, and whole sections. And each time he made such changes he would revise the wording as well.

Anyone seriously interested in literature should make a study of the shaping of *Walden*. Nearly all the original material has been preserved, so one can see how it came into being, bit by bit. The *Journals* were the source of much of it, perhaps even more than we know, for Thoreau would sometimes clip out slips of paper from them and use the words in the ever-growing manuscript.

But interesting as the making of *Walden* is, the finished book is even more fascinating. Thoreau did what few authors have ever even attempted to do. Beneath the surface of what he says are hidden still other things, some of them so well concealed that most readers do not know they exist. This book, which truly belongs to the realm of magic prose, must be read again and again at different ages and in different circumstances for one to grasp even a part of what it has to say. The first encounter may yield comparatively little, but one can return to the book and always find more that was not apparent in earlier readings.

On the surface, *Walden* is an account of the author's two years in the cabin he had built himself for an incredibly low cost. It describes his life there, his relationships with men and animals, the village of Concord, and the passing of the seasons. (The two years are condensed into one to unify the structure of the book.) There are also chapters about reading, sounds, solitude, beans, and many other things, but basically the book deals with the incidents, observations, and thoughts that its author had experienced during his 26 months at Walden Pond. The book is well titled, but the Walden it refers to is far more than a little lake in eastern Massachusetts. His Walden Pond is real enough, but it is also an imaginary place that existed only in the mind of the man who was writing about it. To him, Walden was a symbol, a central core of the natural world that seemed so much better than the artificial world that man had made.

To Thoreau, man's world was a hateful one. His own government had betrayed its people by supporting slavery. His neighbors were so busy trying to get more

money that they had no time for anything else. They
were cutting down the woods, draining the marshlands,
and damming up the rivers. He saw what was happening
and raised his voice in protest. But no one listened; he
was crying to the wind.

The 357-page book that contains the essence of
Thoreau's thinking was published on August 9, 1854.
The proofs Fields wanted to take to England did not
get there, for he was such a poor sailor that he had to
leave the ship at Halifax and return to Boston. As a
result, *Walden* was not issued in Britain for many years.
But some American copies were sent to England where
George Eliot wrote a favorable notice in the *Westmin-
ster Review.*

The American reviews appeared soon after the book
was published. Most of them were quite good, but they
did not create a stir as the controversial notices for
Uncle Tom's Cabin did. The book sold fairly well, certainly far better than *A Week* had. Like Melville's
Moby-Dick, however, it received much less attention
during its author's lifetime than it was to get in the
twentieth century. By that time critics—and the public
—had developed a keener sense of appreciation for fine
literature than Thoreau's and Melville's contemporay
audience had.

With the publication of *Walden,* Thoreau stopped
writing books, although he never gave up planning
them. One of the most ambitious was to be about the
American Indian. He wrote hundreds of pages of notes

for it but never got around to organizing them into a publishable manuscript. Another was to be a treatise on arrowheads that would be illustrated with engravings.

He continued to fill the pages of his *Journal* with material that would one day be put together to make such posthumous books as *Excursions*, *The Maine Woods*, *Cape Cod*, and *A Yankee in Canada*, but *A Week* and *Walden* were the only two of his works that he ever saw published in book form.

Even before *Walden* came off the press, Thoreau's name was evidently known to publishers, for he got a letter from Charles Scribner asking for biographical information for the *Encyclopedia of American Literature*.

In May another fugitive slave case roused Boston. When Anthony Burns was arrested and sent back to slavery, the Abolitionists' attempt at rescue failed, just as it had when Thomas Sims was captured in 1851. At a meeting held in Framingham on July 4 the leader of the activist wing of the Abolitionists, William Lloyd Garrison, denounced the United States Constitution as a proslavery document and burned a copy of it.

Thoreau spoke at this meeting. His speech, "Slavery in Massachusetts," stirred the audience and impressed Garrison so much that he printed it in full in *The Liberator*. So did Greeley in the New York *Tribune*.

What Thoreau said that day still rings with fervor: "Show me a free state, and a court truly of justice, and I will fight for them if need be; but show me Massachusetts, and I refuse her my allegiance and express contempt for her courts. . . . My thoughts are murder to

the State and involuntarily go plotting against her. . . .
We have used up all our inherited freedom. If we would
save our lives we must fight for them. . . . I would side
with the light, and let the dark earth roll from under
me."

He ended his speech on a more positive note. He
described a white water lily that he had recently seen
burst into bloom in Concord. Its sweet scent had particularly impressed him. "What confirmation of our
hopes is in the fragrance of this flower! I shall not so
soon despair of the world for it, notwithstanding slavery
and the cowardice and want of principle of Northern
men. It suggests what kind of laws have prevailed longest, and that the time may come when man's deeds will
smell as sweet. . . . The foul slime [from which it
springs] stands for the sloth and vice of man, the decay
of humanity; the fragrant flower . . . for the purity and
courage which are immortal."

Publication of *Walden* brought not only reviews but
a letter from a New Bedford Quaker named Daniel
Ricketson who wrote to praise the book. Like Harrison
G. O. Blake, he was to be Thoreau's admirer and disci-
ple for the rest of his life.

Like Thoreau, Ricketson had built a small cabin on
some land outside the town and had named his retreat
"The Shanty." When Thoreau came to New Bedford
to lecture, Ricketson insisted that he stay in his home.
After dinner his host made a sketch of Thoreau. It is a
rather amateurish drawing, but it is the only full-length
portrait we have of him. It was not, however, the first

picture made of Thoreau. During the summer, the painter Samuel Worcester Rowse had done a more professional crayon sketch of Thoreau's head while he was boarding in the family home.

Thoreau made another good friend when Thomas Cholmondeley (pronounced "Chumly" as Thoreau said in a letter to Blake), an English gentleman of good family and great wealth, came to Concord to call on Emerson. Since he wanted to stay for some time, he took a room at the Thoreau boardinghouse. Thoreau was so impressed by the generous and cultured Englishman that he took him to Worcester to meet Blake. The three men then went on a walking trip to the top of Mount Wachusett.

When Cholmondeley left Concord to return home he suggested that Thoreau go to England with him. Thoreau, however, did not want to leave his native town and declined the offer.

That autumn Thoreau made a significant entry about himself in his *Journal:*

My faults are:

Paradoxes,—saying just the opposite,—a style which may be imitated.

Ingenious.

Playing with words,—getting the laugh—not always simple, strong, and broad.

Using current phrases and maxims, when I should speak for myself.

Not always earnest.

"In short," "in fact," "alas!" etc.

Want of conciseness.

What he said was all too true. If he had delved deeper, he would have found still other faults of character as well as of expression. But like most of us, he did not allow his self-criticism—especially in writing—to go too far.

THOREAU AND WHITMAN

1856

We visited Whitman . . . and were much interested and provoked.

The winter of 1854–1855 was uneventful for Thoreau. One reason for this was that he was ill most of the time. He did not realize it, but tuberculosis was beginning to make its inroads. During the spring, he was still weak; he tired easily; and he could not get around as well as usual. Nevertheless, he set out with Channing for Cape Cod in July. They stayed there for two weeks but did little exploring.

The illness lingered on through the autumn and kept him depressed in mind as well as in body. Two things happened, though, that served to make his life pleasanter. He received 44 volumes of scarce Oriental books which his friend Thomas Cholmondeley had sent him from England. And during this year a young man named Franklin B. Sanborn moved to Concord to work as a schoolteacher there. Although it was some time before Sanborn and Thoreau became friends, the

younger man was destined to play an important part in
making Thoreau's name better known. He became his
biographer and then edited much of his work. Like
Thoreau, Sanborn was an ardent Abolitionist. This was
to bring them closer together when the struggle against
slavery rose to a climax during the late fifties.

Perhaps Thoreau's long-protracted illness made him
think poorly of himself. In a letter written early in
1856 to a man who had praised *Walden* and wanted to
meet its author he said: "You have the best of me in
my books. . . . I am not worth seeing personally—the
stuttering, blundering, clodhopper that I am."

Fortunately, Thoreau's friends had a higher opinion
of him than he had of himself. Horace Greeley wrote
to invite him to live at his country home in Chappaqua,
New York, where he would be paid for being a tutor
to Greeley's two young children. He was tempted by
the offer but finally refused it.

In June he went to Worcester to visit Blake and other
friends there. During the illness of the previous year he
had grown underchin whiskers—then known as Galway
whiskers—in order to protect his throat from the cold.
They are portrayed in his first photographic portrait,
three of which were made by Benjamin Maxham of
Worcester. The man to whom he had said that he was
"not worth seeing personally" still wanted to get some
idea of what his admired author looked like and therefore sent him the money to pay the photographer. The
daguerreotypes cost 50 cents each.

That summer Thoreau spent some time in New Bedford with Daniel Ricketson and went with him to visit

the nearby island of Naushon. Then he traveled by train to Walpole, New Hampshire, to see Bronson Alcott who had moved there the year before.

Idealistic co-operative settlements like Brook Farm in Massachusetts and the Raritan Bay Union in New Jersey had been popular during the past decade, but they turned out to be financial failures. The Raritan Bay Union at Perth Amboy was about to be transformed into a commuter's development called Eagleswood. A pleasant steamship ride to New York would take the men to work while their wives kept house in the 250-foot long, three-story stone building that had been the co-operative's central dwelling place.

Through Bronson Alcott, who was visiting Eagleswood, Thoreau was employed to make surveys of the new development. He started the work in October.

In November Horace Greeley suggested that Thoreau and Alcott come to his home in Chappaqua to spend a week end there. They stayed only for Saturday, however, and went to Brooklyn on Sunday to hear the famous preacher, Henry Ward Beecher, speak at the Plymouth Church. Thoreau was not impressed. But he did want to meet the poet Walt Whitman, who had written *Leaves of Grass* and had printed it in a shop near the church. Thoreau owned a copy of the book, and he had sent one to Cholmondeley in England. Since Whitman lived on nearby Myrtle Avenue, they decided to call on him. He was not at home, so they returned the next day and at last met the remarkable-looking poet who was two years younger than Thoreau.

He took them upstairs to his untidy room where he
told them "that he loved to ride up and down Broadway
all day on an omnibus, sitting beside the driver, listening
to the roar of the carts, and sometimes gesticulating and
declaiming Homer at the top of his voice." He also said
that he had worked for newspapers, in New Orleans
especially, but that he now had "no employment but to
read and write in the forenoon, and walk in the afternoon, like all the rest of the scribbling gentry."

They continued their conversation downstairs in the
living room. There Thoreau told Whitman that he
thought his works were "wonderfully like the Ori-
entals" and asked if he had read them. "No," said
Whitman forthrightly, "tell me about them."

When they spoke of the recently published second
edition of *Leaves of Grass*, Whitman gave Thoreau a
copy. On the back of the regular edition was stamped a
quotation from a letter from Emerson. It read, in large,
bold letters: "I greet you at the beginning of a great
career." There had been much criticism of Whitman's
making such public use of the phrase, but Thoreau
thought that he successfully defended what he had done.

It was only when the conversation turned to a discus-
sion of the common man that the two writers disagreed.
Thoreau said that he had a low opinion of American
politics and of the way the people were willing to over-
look corruption. Whitman thought that this was "a very
aggravated case of superciliousness." Thoreau, sensing
that what he was saying was "somewhat of a damper"
to Whitman, changed the subject.

Although Whitman had become rather irritated with

his visitor at this point he said later that Thoreau "was a man you would have to like—an interesting man, simple, conclusive." And there is no doubt that Thoreau had been enormously impressed by Whitman. He wrote of him: "He is apparently the greatest democrat the world has ever seen. Kings and aristocrats go by the board at once. . . . A remarkably strong though coarse nature, of a sweet disposition, and much prized by his friends. Though peculiar and rough in his exterior . . . he is essentially a gentleman."

When Thoreau finished reading the second edition of *Leaves of Grass*, which Whitman had inscribed for him, he presented its author with a copy of *A Week*. Of *Leaves of Grass* he said, "It has done me more good than any reading for a long time." He was disturbed by what he called the "sensual" poems, but not by "any brag or egoism in the book." In fact, he said that Whitman "may turn out the least braggart of all, having a better right to be confident."

Thoreau was in good health and in excellent spirits at this time. On December 5 he wrote in his *Journal:* "I have never got over my surprise that I should have been born into the most estimable place in all the world, and in the very nick of time."

Later that month his English friend Cholmondeley began a very long letter to him from Rome. The letter took so much time to write that he did not finish it until two months later in London. In it he gave Thoreau some very serious advice: "You should be a member of some society not yet formed. You want it greatly, and without this you will be liable to moulder away as you get older. *Forgive my English plainness of speech.* Your love for, and intimate acquaintance with, Nature is ancillary to some affection which you have not yet discovered. . . . The lonely man is a diseased man, I greatly fear. See how carefully Mr. Emerson avoids it; and yet, who dwells, in all essentials, more religiously free than he? . . . I wish I lived near you, and that you could somehow originate some such society as I have in my head."

Thoreau, however, did not agree with his friend. A few days before the end of 1856 he confided to his *Journal:* "I thrive best on solitude. If I have had a companion only one day in a week unless it were one or two I could name, I find that the value of the week to me has been seriously affected. It dissipates my days, and often it takes me another week to get over it. . . . I laugh when you tell me of the danger of impoverishing myself by isolation."

Thoreau was evidently satisfied with the way he lived. In January he wrote: "The stones are happy, Concord River is happy, and I am happy too."

The spring of 1857 witnessed national events that were to bring open conflict over slavery nearer. The Supreme Court ruled that Dred Scott, a slave who had sought his liberty because his owner had taken him to free territory, was not entitled to sue in a Federal court. This ruling meant that he was not a man but a thing, a chattel who had no more rights than a cow or a sheep. And this momentous decision came only two days after

James Buchanan was inaugurated President. He was so eager to placate the South that he appointed several Southerners to his Cabinet—and they were men who would soon desert their posts to become high officials in the Confederate government.

Earlier that spring there came to Concord a man who was destined to play a major role in the fight against slavery. Franklin Sanborn brought him to the Thoreau boardinghouse to have lunch. Sanborn proudly introduced him as John Brown. This fierce-looking, outspoken 56-year-old man had come from Kansas where he had fought in the battles against the proslavery forces there. There was blood on his hands, for he and his six sons had slaughtered mercilessly, firm in the belief that the only way to deal with people who favored slaveowning was to kill them outright. But he said nothing about this in Concord, where he wanted to raise money to help his cause.

Sanborn had to leave the luncheon table to return to school, but Brown stayed on, telling Thoreau more and more about affairs in Kansas. When he spoke at the Town Hall that night he showed his listeners a big bowie knife he had found on one of the proslavery men. Then he displayed a chain that they had used when they captured one of his sons. He also told the audience that one son had been killed and another driven insane by the border ruffians who wanted to make sure that Kansas would become a slave state.

Thoreau did not often contribute to causes, but he and Sanborn and Emerson were among those who gave money to Brown that night. Thoreau, poor as he was, might have given more but he was put out that Brown did not trust anyone enough to explain what his future plans were. Nevertheless he said in his *Journal* that he had great confidence in the man from Kansas.

He introduced John Brown to Emerson who invited him to his house. There Thoreau saw him again and was even more impressed by him. After that, Brown went off to solicit more funds in other New England towns.

THOREAU AND
JOHN BROWN

1859

I would rather see the statue of Captain Brown in the Massachusetts State-House yard than that of any other man whom I know. I rejoice that I live in this age, that I am his contemporary.

Except for Thoreau's brief encounter with John Brown in Concord, the year 1857 was not a notable one for him. He went to Cape Cod in June and to Maine in July. During the fall, he became ill again and let his beard grow longer in order to protect his throat better. With the oncoming of winter his fingers failed him so badly that he could hardly tie his shoelaces. He was forty years old and keenly aware of it.

Nor was 1858 much better. The year seemed to begin well when James Russell Lowell, editor of the recently founded *Atlantic Monthly*, asked him for an article. Thoreau sent Lowell about a hundred pages of manuscript he had written about his trips to the Maine woods. Meanwhile, he went on a short visit to New York and then on another to New Hampshire.

When he returned to Concord in June he got a copy of the *Atlantic Monthly* with the first installment of the Maine woods article in it. Then, when he received the July installment, he was surprised to find that a sentence—which had been cut out in the proofs and which he had asked to be restored—was still omitted in the printed version. It was a harmless enough sentence, one that implied that a tree might be as immortal as a man and thus go to Heaven with him, but Thoreau was outraged because such liberties had been taken with his prose. He wrote Lowell a long letter about it in which he said, "I am not willing to be associated in any way, unneccessarily, with parties who will confess themselves so bigoted & timid as this implies."

Thoreau had to dun Lowell for payment for the pieces he had printed. Then he refused to have any more dealings with the *Atlantic* until a new editor took Lowell's place in 1861.

In July, Thoreau went on another trip through the White Mountains, this time by horse and carriage and accompanied by Edward Hoar, who had been with him when they accidentally set fire to the Concord woods. They climbed Mount Washington, where Thoreau did amazingly well for a man who had been so ill the year before. In a sheltered ravine where there was still snow he tore his nails in an effort to keep from sliding down the steep slope there. Then he sprained his ankle so badly while jumping from rock to rock that he could not sleep that night or walk the next day. Fortunately, he had found some healing herbs which he used to ease the pain. He also immersed his foot in the ice-cold mountain water to reduce the swelling.

They remained on the mountain for several days, spending most of their time botanizing. They also climbed Mount Lafayette and were impressed by the sight of the other great mountains in the vicinity of Mount Washington.

In September, Thoreau went to Cape Ann for a few days, eating bread, herring, and tea to economize. Since he made most of the journey on foot he also saved money on transportation costs.

During the late summer and autumn of 1858 the newspapers were reporting a series of debates that were taking place in Illinois between the well-known Stephen A. Douglas and the still-obscure Springfield attorney, Abraham Lincoln. In this campaign for a seat in the United States Senate, the two men concentrated their attention on the important issue of slavery being extended into newly settled territory. Douglas won the election, but what Lincoln had said during the debates brought him national fame.

Thoreau paid no attention to what Lincoln was saying. The Abolitionists had no use for anyone with moderate views about slavery. Merely to oppose its extension into the territories was not enough.

In December, Thomas Cholmondeley visited Concord again. The well-traveled Englishman, who was on his way to the West Indies, wanted to see the whaling industry at New Bedford, so Thoreau took him there to meet Ricketson. Cholmondeley invited Thoreau to accompany him to the Caribbean, but Thoreau, of course, had no desire to leave Concord.

He could not have gone at this time, even if he had wanted to, because his father had had jaundice in October and was now coughing constantly. When the ailing man could not leave his bedroom, Thoreau took care of him and was his nurse until he died on February 3 at the age of seventy-one.

His death meant that Thoreau officially became the head of the house and had to take full charge of the graphite business. Again he improved the methods of manufacture.

It was apparent, however, that he personally was not earning much at this time. When the Harvard College Library wrote to him, soliciting funds for the purchase of books, Thoreau sent five dollars and said that "I would gladly give more, but this exceeds my income from all sources together for the last four months."

He continued to lecture, speaking in Concord, Worcester, and Lynn, among other places, but, as he had long since learned, the income from a few speaking engagements was not enough to pay his living expenses. Yet the year 1859 was a good one for lecturing, the best he had ever had.

In May, John Brown, mysterious as ever about his activities, came to Concord again to speak at the Town Hall in an effort to raise more money for the anti-slavery cause. Since Brown was staying with Sanborn, who was completely convinced of the old man's sincerity, Thoreau naturally was led to believe that what he was doing was all for the best even though he would still not reveal his plans.

During the summer, Thoreau was employed by the local government to make a detailed survey of the Concord River. He found this work much more to his liking than making routine measurements of private parcels of land. As a result he spent many weeks determining the river's course, depth, and rate of flow, as well as recording the dimensions of its bridges and dams.

The summer passed quietly, and the leaves began to turn into the vivid colors that presage the coming of winter. Thoreau was particularly interested in leaf coloration at this time. He had written a piece entitled "Autumnal Tints," which he was using as the basis for a lecture. When Theodore Parker's church in Boston wanted him to speak there, Emerson suggested that he use this. But Thoreau wrote to say that he thought that "Life Without Principle" was better suited to a church. He spoke there to an appreciative audience on October 9. Then, just a week later, news came over the telegraph wires that shattered the peace of Concord.

Thoreau was at Emerson's house when word arrived. The government arsenal at Harpers Ferry in Virginia had been raided by John Brown, his sons, a few trusted white men, and five Negro slaves whom he had pressed into service, telling them that they must strike a blow for their own freedom. The first reports erroneously said that Brown had been killed, but there was no doubt that his attack on the arsenal had failed.

During the next few days, more and more details became known. Captain Robert E. Lee and a company of marines had put down the invasion of the arsenal and had killed or captured most of the men involved in it. Brown was not dead but wounded, and had been put in the nearby Charles Town jail which was under heavy guard.

Thoreau was disgusted at the reaction in Concord. The postmaster, thinking that Brown had been killed, announced that "he died as the fool dieth." Others said that Brown was "undoubtedly insane," or that "it served him right."

Thoreau did not approve of violence and would never use it himself, but he believed that keeping human beings in slavery was so wrong that any means—even forcible ones—should be used against it. To him John Brown was a martyr.

When the words that Brown spoke while lying wounded on the floor of the enginehouse at Harpers Ferry were published, Thoreau became even more convinced about the rightness of the old fighter's deed. "No man sent me here," Brown said when accused of having had others give him support. "It was my own prompting and that of my Maker. I acknowledge no master in human form."

Thoreau wrote in his *Journal* what the prisoner had said:

"I pity the poor in bondage that have none to help them; that is why I am here; not to gratify any personal animosity, revenge, or vindictive spirit. It is my sympathy with the oppressed and the wronged, that are as good as you, and as precious in the sight of God.

"I want you to understand that I respect the rights of the poorest and the weakest of colored people, oppressed by the slave system, just as much as I do those of the most wealthy and powerful.

"I wish to say, furthermore, that you had better, all you people at the South, prepare yourselves for a settlement of that question that must come up for settlement sooner than you are prepared for it. The sooner you are prepared the better. You may dispose of me very easily. I am nearly disposed of now; but this question is still to be settled—this Negro question, I mean; the end of that is not yet."

For days Thoreau kept putting down in his *Journal* his thoughts about John Brown and slavery. He did not, however, make a day-by-day record of what was happening in the trial that was being held in Charles Town. His *Journal* entries provided material for speeches— and he had never been so eager to have an audience before.

He asked for the use of the Concord Town Hall for a meeting on October 30. As a citizen of the town, he could not be refused the right to use the building, but the selectman could and did forbid him to ring the great bell to summon people. Thoreau ignored them; he seized the bell rope, pulled it again and again, making its mighty clamor roll out over the quiet streets of the town.

He got an audience, but much of it was hostile. What he said on that memorable night was later printed as "A Plea for Captain John Brown." He had never been so forceful, so moving, so stirred with emotion.

He was speaking, he said, to correct the erroneous and unjust statements that had appeared in the news-

papers. He told the audience that even William Lloyd
Garrison's Abolitionist *Liberator* had come out against
Brown. Then he outlined the old freedom fighter's life,
described Brown's Spartan personal habits, and called
him a Transcendentalist. He was there not to plead
John Brown's cause, he said, but his character, for the
man had a spark of divinity in him. He was "such a man
as it takes ages to make and ages to understand. . . . a
man such as the sun may not rise upon again . . . sent
to be the redeemer of those in captivity; and the only
use to which you can put him is to hang him at the end
of a rope!"

Nevertheless, he added, "I see now that it is necessary
that the bravest and most humane man in all the country
should be hung. Perhaps he saw it himself. I *almost fear*
that I may yet hear of his deliverance, doubting if a
prolonged life, if *any* life, can do as much good as his
death."

Thoreau mentioned the idea of "deliverance" because
he knew that several plots were under way to rescue
Brown from the Charles Town jail and spirit him away.
They came to nothing because the building was heavily
guarded—and John Brown himself discouraged any attempt at rescue.

Toward the end of his speech, Thoreau quoted what
Brown had said while lying wounded on the enginehouse floor. They were stirring words. Those in the
audience who had come to jeer left quietly.

What Thoreau said that night in Concord attracted
attention. He was asked to speak in Boston to replace
the Negro Abolitionist, Frederick Douglass, who had

intended to address an audience there but who had to flee to Canada when evidence that connected him with John Brown was discovered. The big hall at Tremont Temple was filled, and the Boston newspapers reported the speech at length. Thoreau spoke again at Worcester and then prepared for a meeting at Concord, for John Brown had been sentenced to death and was to be hanged in public on December 2.

On November 30, Thoreau wrote in his *Journal* that he was one of a committee of four, including Emerson, a former governor, and a former high sheriff, chosen to ask the selectmen to have the bell of the First Parish Church tolled while Brown was being hanged. Permission was refused, and Thoreau was told that 500 of his fellow townsmen were damning him for his actions and that if he rang the bell they would fire cannon.

As a result the memorial service was a quiet one. Thoreau spoke and read poems by Andrew Marvell and Sir Walter Raleigh. He concluded his brief address with a translation he had made from Tacitus. It dealt with the death of Agricola. "Whatever of Agricola we have loved," Tacitus had said, "whatever we have admired, remains, and will remain, in the minds of men and the records of history, through the eternity of ages."

One of Brown's men—Francis Jackson Merriam— had escaped and was in Boston. Fear and excitement had unhinged his mind. He had been persuaded to take a train to Canada, where he would be safe, but by error took one that ended its run at Concord. There he went to Sanborn's house for refuge.

Sanborn was too closely connected with the Brown

affair to be caught in the company of a man who had
been in the Harpers Ferry raid, so he asked Emerson
for the use of his horse and wagon, and requested
Thoreau to take Merriam to the next station on the line
and put him on a train there. When the two men
started out the next morning, Thoreau soon found out
that his companion was insane. He kept insisting that
Thoreau was Emerson and babbled on during the four-
mile ride. At one time he jumped out and had to be
talked into returning to the wagon. Sanborn had not
told Thoreau who the man was or why he was so distraught. But it was evident from what he said that he
had been with John Brown. Thoreau finally got him to
the train.

So far as Concord was concerned the John Brown
case had not ended. Thoreau was being urged to write
a life of him, but he said that he was too involved with
his Indian studies at this time. A journalist, James Red-
path, was planning, however, to write one. Meanwhile,
he was putting together a collection of the many articles
the event had inspired. It was to be called *Echoes of
Harpers Ferry*, and the royalties it earned were to go
to Brown's family. Thoreau's speech, "A Plea for Captain John Brown," was to be included. The book was
dedicated to Thoreau, Emerson, and Wendell Phillips.
It sold very well when it came out early in 1860, for
there was still great interest in the celebrated case.

A Senate investigating committee kept the interest
alive as it uncovered more and more details of the way
the Harpers Ferry raid had been planned. Among those

summoned to Washington was Franklin Sanborn. He refused to go, and was then served with a subpoena by a deputy United States marshal and his four assistants. They got into the Sanborn home by a ruse, seized him, and tried to take him out of the house. There was a terrific struggle that brought scores of townspeople running to the scene. Among them was Thoreau.

Judge Samuel Hoar, the father of Edward Hoar, issued a writ of habeas corpus which ordered the officers to let Sanborn go. When they tried to appeal to the people of Concord, the enraged crowd turned on them and drove them out of town.

On the following day, Sanborn was taken to Boston to appear before a hastily called session of the State Supreme Court, which discharged him from arrest. On his return to Concord, he found the town wildly celebrating. A meeting was held at the Town Hall at which both Emerson and Thoreau spoke. John Brown's death had changed public opinion in Concord. The lines were hardening, and the fight against slavery was being brought out into the open. Only a war could settle it now.

John Brown had been buried on his farm near North Elba in the Adirondacks. A memorial meeting was held there on July 4, 1860, to which Thoreau was invited. He could not go, but he did write a paper, "The Last Days of John Brown," that was read during the ceremonies. It told how opinion had changed in favor of Brown as more and more people realized that what he had done was a heroic act. In conclusion, he said:

Of all the men who were said to be my contemporaries, it seemed to me that John Brown was the only one who *had not died.* . . . He is more alive than he ever was. He has earned immortality. He is not confined to North Elba nor to Kansas. He is no longer working in secret. He works in public, and in the clearest light that shines on this land.

Before the next year was out, Northern soldiers were parading through the streets of Boston, singing words which they took into battle:

> John Brown's body lies a-mouldering in the grave,
> His soul goes marching on.

THE YEARS BETWEEN

1859-1861

To the sick the doctors wisely recommend a change of air and scenery.

At the beginning of the speech Thoreau wrote to be read at the John Brown memorial services in North Elba, he said, "For my own part, I commonly attend more to nature than to man." This was becoming very true. From now on the *Journal* entries have far more to do with natural phenomena than they do with people and their activities. The few that refer to human affairs are usually harsh and bitter. On May 2, 1860, he wrote: "A crowd of men seem to generate vermin even of the human kind. In great towns there is degradation undreamed of elsewhere—gamblers, dog-killers, ragpickers. Some live by robbery or luck."

And then the *Journal* goes on with page after page devoted to plants, fish, animals, water temperature, and other observations of field and stream but with very little about the people Thoreau knew.

Hawthorne had returned to Concord in June, and

147

much was happening on the national scene that was of tremendous importance. In May, Abraham Lincoln was nominated as the Republican candidate for President, something that was bringing dire threats from the South about seceding from the Union in the unlikely event that he was elected. Thoreau obviously was aware of what was happening, but he hardly ever mentioned it in his *Journal* or his letters.

Yet 1860 was an exceedingly important year in many ways. The census showed that the United States then had a population of 31,443,321 of whom 3,953,760 were Negro slaves, while 488,070 black people were free. The North had more than 19 million people, while the South had hardly more than 12 million. The South was becoming restless, because it was evident that the far more prosperous and better-populated North would soon control the national government.

Changes of all kinds were under way. Thoreau was fascinated by one account of them. Charles Darwin's book, *The Origin of Species*, had just been published in England, and Thoreau had obtained one of the first copies to arrive in America. Ideas about evolution had been in the shaping for some time, but here at last was a work by an eminent scientist which cast new light on the way all living things—including man—had changed over long periods of time until they had assumed the forms they have today.

Very little happened to Thoreau during this year. He wrote relatively few letters, and those he did write are, with some exceptions, lacking in interest. He replied to a young man who had sent him a long, dull poem about the Concord Fight and told him not to try to have it printed. "The public are very cold and indifferent to such things, and the publishers even more so," he said. "I have found that the precept 'Write with fury, and correct with flegm' required me to print only the hundredth part of what I have written. . . . You may think this harsh advice, but, believe me, it is sincere."

There was some lecturing and a trip to Mount Monadnock with Channing in August, while writing, of course, went on all the time, although it consisted only of *Journal* entries and Nature articles that could be used on the platform and perhaps be published later in some magazine.

In August a twenty-three-year-old journalist who was to make a name for himself in American letters arrived in Concord with a letter from James Russell Lowell introducing him to Hawthorne. This was William Dean Howells. He was coming down from the north in one of the stagecoaches that were fast disappearing from the countryside. Along the way he had been greatly impressed by the scenery. "The meadows were newly mown, and the air was fragrant with the grass," he wrote in an article about his experiences in New England. "The land was lovelier than any I had ever seen, with its old farmhouses, and brambled gray stone walls, its stony hillsides, its staggering orchards, its wooded tops, and its thick-brackened valleys."

After spending some time with Hawthorne, Howells wanted to see Thoreau and Emerson. He describes his meeting with Thoreau: "He came into the room a quaint, stump figure of a man, whose effect of long

trunk and short limbs was heightened by his fashionless
trousers being let down too low. He had a noble face,
with tossed hair, a distraught eye, and a fine aquilinity
of profile. . . ."

Thoreau gave Howells a chair on one side of the
room while he seated himself on the other side. The
distance between them typified the meeting. Howells
was young and inexperienced; Thoreau was more than
usually reserved and reticent. Howells tried to question
him about Walden Pond and John Brown, which the
young reporter even then realized were the two most
important experiences in Thoreau's life, but the replies
he got—with long pauses between statements—were
"vague, orphic phrases."

"It was not merely a defeat of my hopes, it was a
rout," Howells wrote; and he was an admirer of
Thoreau's writings and of John Brown. He went on to
visit Emerson, whom he found somewhat easier to talk
to.

At this time Thoreau was far more interested in trees
than he was in reporters who wanted to use him as a
subject. He was one of the first to realize that the age
of trees can be determined by counting their annual
growth-rings—an idea that was to become formalized
in the modern science of dendrochronology. And he
was also a pioneer in establishing our knowledge of the
way various species of trees replace one another when a
forest is cut down. In September he read "The Success-
sion of Forest Trees" to an audience in the Concord
Town Hall and had the entire article published the next
month in Greeley's *Weekly Tribune*.

Even his friends were not immune to Thoreau's growing hostility to people. On November 4 he wrote a long
and rather harsh letter to Daniel Ricketson, with whom
he had been on good terms for many years. He was
annoyed because Ricketson had reproached him for not
writing oftener. "You know that I never promised to
correspond with you," he said. "I rarely go abroad, and
it is quite a habit with me to decline invitations to do
so. . . . I am very busy, after my fashion, little as there
is to show for it, and feel as if I could not spend many
days nor dollars in travelling." But he ended the letter
on a more kindly note: "Please remember me to your
family. I have a very pleasant recollection of your fire-
side, and I trust that I shall revisit it—also of your
shanty and the surrounding regions."

Two days after this letter, Abraham Lincoln was
elected the first Republican President of the United
States. It was a crucial election, one that was to plunge
the nation into war, but Thoreau ignored it in his
Journal and his letters. He was used to seeing a suc-
cession of mediocre men become President, and he
naturally assumed that Lincoln was another one of them.
In fact, the exceedingly cautious way that Lincoln be-
haved during the months between being elected and
taking office gave Thoreau no reason to believe that the
President-elect had any ability at all.

Early in December, Thoreau's intense interest in trees
had an unfortunate outcome. He went out in bad
weather to measure tree growth-rings and caught a cold
that rapidly developed into what he called bronchitis.
Then he made the condition worse by insisting on going
to Waterbury, Connecticut, on December 11 to keep a

lecture date. He was feeling miserable when he arrived, and the lecture went so badly that the local newspaper called it dull. When he returned to Concord, he was so ill that he could not leave the house for a good part of the winter. He did not know it, but the final stages of tuberculosis had set in.

The cold, wintry days passed. On December 20, South Carolina seceded from the Union, and the nation rushed headlong into civil war, but Thoreau, sick and confined to the house, did not notice or even seem to care.

One by one the Southern states seized Federal forts and arsenals, and began to follow South Carolina out of the Union. Then, in February, the provisional government of the Confederate States of America was formed in Montgomery, Alabama, and Jefferson Davis was made its president. On March 4, Abraham Lincoln was inaugurated as President of the United States, and a tense country waited to see what would happen.

On Inauguration Day, Thoreau told Bronson Alcott that he was "impatient with the politicians, the state of the country, the State itself, and with statesmen generally." He apparently could not understand the true significance of what was going on. Yet he was getting better, at least a little better. By March 22 he was able to write to Daniel Ricketson. He made no mention of national events and spoke only of his illness, the weather, and some of the people they both knew.

Alcott, who had become the superintendent of Concord's public schools, was trying to persuade Thoreau to write a book about Concord that could be used in the classrooms. Thoreau, however, was not well enough to undertake such work. He was just beginning to be able to walk through the streets of the town on days when the weather was good. By early April he had recovered sufficiently to take a two-mile walk.

Thoreau's doctor, however, was still worried about his health. Perhaps a warmer climate would help—the West Indies, Europe, anywhere with a mild climate. One of Thoreau's Maine cousins had gone to Minnesota and had found that he felt better in its crisp dry air. Perhaps Minnesota should be the place. It had Indians to be observed and written about, and the newly admitted state also had plenty of wild country to be explored.

He could not go there alone. He tried to persuade Channing and then Blake to accompany him, but neither of them felt free to go on such a long trip. There was one other possibility, seventeen-year-old Horace Mann, Jr. His father, the noted educator, had died recently, and he was living in Concord with his mother. He was interested in natural history; he admired Thoreau and had often visited him during his illness. Not only was he available—he was eager to go.

They made plans quickly and paid no attention to the fact that the nation was already at war. Fort Sumter in Charleston Harbor had been fired on and then had surrendered to the Confederates on April 14. The new President was calling for militia to serve for three months. It was thought that this would surely be time enough to put down a rebellion by a few Southern states that did not have weapons or the money to buy them.

THE LAST LONG
JOURNEY, MINNESOTA

1861

Start now on that farthest way, which does not pause at the Mississippi or the Pacific . . . but leads on direct a tangent to this sphere, summer and winter, day and night, sun down, noon down, and at last earth down too.

They left Concord by train on May 11, stopped over at Worcester for two days to see Blake, and then went on to Albany and Niagara Falls. Thoreau made brief entries in his *Journal* for the first four days and then stopped for a long while. The *Journal* that had been kept with such care for 24 years was now nearly finished. The 1400-mile journey to Minnesota was the beginning of the end.

They waited at Niagara Falls for five days because there was a chance that Channing might join them there. But he, undependable as ever, did not show up, so they went on to Detroit and Chicago.

Emerson had given Thoreau some letters of introduction to people living in places they would pass through. He used one in Chicago to call on a Unitarian minister and was cordially received by him. Evidently there was

some talk about Thoreau's writing a book about the
West, but his book-writing days were over. He tired
easily and found traveling difficult. As usual, he was
particularly interested in the plants, birds, and animals
he encountered along the way.

After they left Chicago, he saw the Mississippi River
for the first time when they took a steamer to go up-
stream to St. Paul, Minnesota. He describes a boat
landing:

Every town has a wharf, with one storage building (or
several) on it, and as many hotels. . . . Perhaps there will
be a heap of sacks filled with wheat on the natural jetty
or levee close by; or, above Dubuque and Dunleith, a blue
sack of pig lead. . . .

The steamer approaching whistles, then strikes a bell
about six times funereally . . . and then you see the whole
village making haste to the landing . . . the postmaster with
his mailbag, the passenger, and almost every dog and pig in
town.

They arrived at St. Paul on May 26 and then spent a
week in St. Anthony and Minneapolis. At Fort Snelling
they saw hundreds of volunteers drilling. When Thoreau
wrote to Sanborn he said that "the people of Minnesota
have *seemed* to me more cold—to feel less implicated
in this war—than the people of Massachusetts." He was
at last becoming aware of the preparations for battle
that were going on throughout the entire country.

He was not too ill to make short trips into the countryside to observe the flora and fauna in a land that was
entirely new to him. Apparently he was well enough
by the middle of June to travel by steamboat up the

Minnesota River to see a meeting of the Sioux Indians
at Redwood. The voyage up that narrow stream was a
new experience for him:

In making a short turn, we repeatedly and designedly
ran into the steep and soft bank, taking in a cart-load of
earth, this being more effectual than the rudder to fetch
us about again. . . . There was not a straight reach a mile
in length . . . generally you could not see a quarter of mile
of water, & the boat was steadily turning this way or that.
. . . The boat was about 160 feet long & drew some 3 feet
of water, or, often water and sand. . . . We very frequently
got aground and then drew ourselves along with a wind-
lass & cable fastened to a tree, or we swung around in the
current, and completely blocked up the stream, one end
of the boat resting on each shore.

After three days of such river travel they arrived at
the Sioux Agency at Redwood. It was "a mere locality"
on great plains that stretched for miles with no trees in
sight. Buffalo were said to be only a score of miles away.

Many Indians had ridden to the council from homes
scattered across the prairie. During the afternoon they
staged a dance at the request of the governor of Minnesota. In the ceremony, Thoreau said, "were 30 men
dancing, and twelve musicians with drums; others struck
their arrows against their bows. Some dancers blew
flutes and kept good time, moving their feet or their
shoulders—sometimes one, sometimes both. They wore
no shirts."

Thoreau probably wanted to stay longer, but the
steamer was returning, and there was no other way to
get back. The unmarked prairie would be dangerous to

cross on foot, for rattlesnakes were common there. And the Indians, who had seemed so peaceful at Redwood, were actually on the edge of revolt. A year later they did go on the warpath, led by Little Crow, a chief whom Thoreau had been impressed by at the ceremonial dance. He wrote then that the Indians "were quite dissatisfied with the white man's treatment of them and probably have reason to be so." More than eight hundred settlers were killed in a bloody uprising the next year.

Redwood was the farthest point in Thoreau's journey to the West. They had planned on being away for three months, but even before they went on their expedition to the Indians, young Horace Mann had written to his mother to expect them home early in July.

A good part of the return trip was made on steamers through the Great Lakes. Thoreau found it far easier to travel on them than on the rather crude trains of the time. They arrived in Concord on July 9, three days before Thoreau's forty-fourth birthday.

It was evident that his health was worse than when he had begun the journey. And he knew how bad it was. He no longer bothered with his *Journal*, and he wrote very few letters. In one of them he said to Daniel Ricketson:

I returned a few weeks ago, after a good deal of steady travelling, considerably, yet not essentially better, my cough still continuing. If I do not mend quickly I shall be obliged to go to another climate again very soon. My ordinary pursuits, both indoor and out, have been for the most part omitted or seriously interrupted—walking, boating, scrib-

bling, &. Indeed I have been sick so long that I have almost
forgotten what it is to be well.

Yet he evidently felt well enough to travel to New
Bedford to spend five days with Ricketson. During that
time he had an ambrotype made by the local photographer. It shows him with a full beard and a rather
tired face.

A few weeks later Ricketson had a "water-cure"
doctor examine Thoreau. He permitted this only to
please his friend, for he had no confidence in doctors,
certainly not in a hydropath. From now on he refused
to have anything to do with healers of any kind. Let
nature take its course. There was no fending off man's
allotted destiny.

Late in September he walked to Walden Pond for the
last time. The wild grapes were ripening, and their
fragrance filled the autumn air. He picked a few and
dropped them into the water.

His well-to-do neighbors, the Hoars, lent him the use
of their horse and cart so he could go out to see country
he could no longer cover on foot. Their dog went along
regularly, looking forward to each short trip with eager
anticipation.

Then the winter set in, and there was no more going
outdoors for a man who had once spent most of his
time there. He settled down quietly in the house, gradually growing weaker as his hacking cough became
worse. The stairs to his attic quarters were too much for
him, so he stayed in the living room, sleeping there on
his day bed.

A MORNING IN MAY

1862

Time is but the stream I go a-fishing in. I drink at it; but while I drink I see the sandy bottom and detect how shallow it is. Its thin current slides away, but eternity remains. I would drink deeper; fish in the sky, whose bottom is pebbly with stars.

The Yellow House, where Thoreau was slowly dying, is on Main Street not far from the center of Concord. Through the parlor window he could see people passing and get a glimpse of carriages and wagons as they drove by. He knew nearly everyone he saw. Some people stopped in to talk with him.

As winter advanced, and snow covered the streets, wheeled vehicles were replaced by sleighs. Bells mounted on the horses' harness jangled and played merry tunes in the crisp cold air. Foot passers-by were bundled up, and they were usually in a hurry to get where they were going. All sounds, except the sleigh bells, were muffled. The town was covered by white silence.

Just before Christmas an attack of pleurisy made

matters worse for the ailing man. But he recovered and
seemed cheerful. He talked to his friends and had lost
none of his interest in the natural world he could not
go out to see.

Ricketson, not realizing how very ill Thoreau was,
wrote to say that he was always welcome if he wanted
to come to New Bedford at any time. Alcott had to
write a reply:

He grows feebler day by day and is evidently failing
and fading from our sight. He gets some sleep, has a pretty
good appetite, reads at intervals, takes notes of his readings,
and likes to see his friends, conversing, however with diffi-
culty, as his voice partakes of his general debility.

Although Thoreau was able to hold a pencil to scrib-
ble his own notes, he could not manage a pen well
enough to write letters for others to read. His sister
Sophia became his devoted secretary.

He had made only a few scattered entries in his
Journal after his trip to Minnesota. One of the longest
and most interesting describes the activities of four
kittens that had just been born in the Thoreau house.
(He always liked cats and often recounted their doings
in his writings.) Then on November 3, 1861, he made
the very last entry in the thirty-ninth volume of the
long record of his life. At that time he was still able to
walk and had gone to the railroad cut near Walden
Pond. There had been a storm during the night, and he
was interested in noting that the pelting raindrops had
left deep marks in the gravel that indicated exactly the
direction from which the rain had come. The last words

are: "All this is perfectly distinct to an observant eye, and yet could easily pass unnoticed by most. Thus each wind is self-registering."

Now that wonderfully observant eye was dimming. But with his sister's help he could still do some literary work. In February came the chance to do so. The publisher of *Walden*, Ticknor and Fields, had taken over the *Atlantic Monthly* in 1859, and James Russell Lowell was no longer its editor. When Fields asked Thoreau for some contributions, the often-offended writer was still cautious even though Lowell would not be involved. There must be no changes in his copy, he insisted. What would the rate of payment be? And was the magazine copyrighted?

When Ticknor made him a good offer and assured him that he would be well treated, Thoreau began immediately to prepare the often-given lecture "Autumnal Tints" for the press. For a while he could use the pencil to make notes for his sister to copy by pen. When he was no longer able to do that, he dictated. He was eager to get the work done, for the money from the *Atlantic* would go to the family, and his writings would appear in print.

This time the relationship between publisher and author was a good one. Ticknor and Fields took over the 596 bound and unbound copies of *A Week on the Concord and Merrimack Rivers* and also agreed to issue a second edition of *Walden*. They printed 280 copies, but finished books did not come out of the bindery in time for Thoreau to see a copy.

One thing he wanted to make sure of was that the

subtitle, *Life in the Woods*, should be omitted. It was, although many later editions still continue to use it.

Soon after this he sent the *Atlantic* the lecture he had often given under the title "The Higher Law," but Fields did not like the phrase. Thoreau changed it to "Life Without Principle," which is what we call it today. Then he sent two more essays, "Walking" and "Wild Apples." All this material, of course, had been written years before; he was in no condition to do anything new and had trouble enough revising the old pieces.

Fields brought Thoreau some publicity by commissioning Bronson Alcott to write a sketch entitled "The Forester" which appeared in the April *Atlantic*. It did not use Thoreau's name, but the verse at the end made it clear who was meant when it said that the Forester had "built himself a little Hermitage" by "blue-eyed Walden."

By April, Thoreau was very near to death. Sophia wrote to Ricketson that "for many weeks he has spoken only in a faint whisper. Henry accepts this dispensation with such childlike trust and is so happy that I feel as if he were being translated rather than dying in the way of most mortals."

The end was very close now. Friends came to see him. Emerson was often there, and one day Sam Staples, the man who had jailed Thoreau, called at the house. He was evidently impressed, for he said to Emerson that he had never seen "a man dying with so much pleasure and peace." Hawthorne also came, bringing his music box because he knew that Thoreau had always liked its tunes.

His Aunt Louisa wanted to know whether he had

made his peace with God. "I did not know that we had ever quarrelled," he said with a wry smile.

During these spring months of 1862, the war that was to free the slaves was going badly for the North. A new general, George B. McClellan, had been put in charge of the army. His plan was to attack the Confederate capital, Richmond, but he was so slow getting under way that the public was becoming impatient. Things were better farther south, where the grimly determined naval commander, David Glasgow Farragut, took the Federal fleet up the Mississippi and captured New Orleans on April 25.

All this seemed very far away to the dying man in the parlor of the Yellow House. But he was keenly aware that spring had arrived and that the sunshine was warmer. Through the window he could see leaves coming out and sometimes could catch a glimpse of one of the birds that were now appearing in Concord.

Channing and Alcott called to see him on May 4 and 5 and probably expected to call again on the sixth. But early that morning the end came, so quietly that the dying man simply faded away. By nine o'clock he was dead. His last words were "moose . . . Indian"; he had probably been revisiting the Maine woods in his last sleep.

Thoreau had not been a member of the First Parish Church and had refused to pay taxes to it. But it was his family's church, and Emerson, who was to read the eulogy, wanted the funeral services to be held there.

And so they were, on the afternoon of May ninth. Nearly all the people Thoreau had known well—his family, Hawthorne, Channing, Alcott, Fields, and Blake —were present when Emerson read the long paper he had written for the occasion. He ended with these words:

The country knows not yet . . . how great a son it has lost. . . . His soul was made for the noblest society; he had in a short life exhausted the capabilities of this world; wherever there is knowledge, wherever there is virtue, wherever there is beauty, he will find a home.

THE AFTER YEARS

1862-

Every day a new picture is painted and framed, held up for half an hour, in such lights as the Great Artist chooses, and then withdrawn, and the curtain falls. And then the sun goes down, and long the afterglow gives light. And then the damask curtains glow along the western window. And now the first star is lit, and I go home.

During the years following Thoreau's death his sister Sophia, Ellery Channing, and Emerson collected his articles and *Journal* entries for publication in several volumes. Until 1866, when *A Yankee in Canada* was issued, a steady stream of books bearing Thoreau's name kept coming from the press. Then there was a long period of silence which was not broken until 1881, when Thoreau's friend, H. G. O. Blake compiled the first of four volumes on the seasons from material in the *Journals*.

In the natural course of events it was to be expected that Thoreau's works would gradually disappear from the market and that he would be forgotten as a good many of his contemporaries have been. But there was enough interest in his writings for Houghton Mifflin, the successors of Ticknor and Fields, to bring out their eleven-volume Riverside Edition in 1893–1894. In 1906, they issued an even more complete collection, the Walden Edition, which included fourteen volumes of the *Journal*. Since then, books by and about Thoreau have kept appearing although there was a lull during the 1920's.

The Depression years caused a revival of interest in an author who spoke out for the common man and was very much concerned with the economics of earning a living.

The decade between 1940 and 1950 showed a great increase in the number of scholarly works on Thoreau. Not only in America but in other countries people were writing about him and translating his books and articles. Publishers in England, France, Germany, Holland, Denmark, Sweden, Finland, Czechoslovakia, Italy, Latin America, Israel, and India brought out Thoreau books. He became especially popular in Japan, where *Walden* has been translated a number of times and a biography of its author has been published. More than 200 editions of *Walden* have been printed in various countries throughout the world.

The rise of "Civil Disobedience" to fame began in 1900 when Leo Tolstoy, the noted Russian writer, sent a letter to the *North American Review* in which he advised Americans to listen to what Thoreau had said rather than follow the precepts of the military-industrial complex that even then dominated the country's thinking.

At about the same time Mohandas K. Gandhi, a young student from India, read the essay while he was at Oxford. He took a copy of it to South Africa when he began to practice law there and printed it in 1907 in a newspaper he was publishing. His followers took Thoreau's advice and began a successful campaign of passive resistance. Word of what they were doing soon spread to other lands. It has been on the march ever since.

"Civil Disobedience" became an inspiration to the Danish resistance to the Nazis in the Second World War. It also helped to influence the black revolution in America, particularly Martin Luther King, Jr., who said on reading the essay: "I became convinced then that non-cooperation with evil is as much a moral obligation as is cooperation with good. . . . The teachings of Thoreau are alive today, indeed, they are more alive today than ever before."

Today Thoreau has become a major figure in world literature. And he is becoming noted as a prose stylist as well as an advocate of much that is now foremost in people's thinking. He more than any of his contemporaries—Emerson, Hawthorne, Melville, Poe, or even Whitman—speaks not only for his time but for ours. His is the voice that predicted what would happen when our forests were cut down and the countryside ravaged. He denounced the moneygrubbers of his day and showed how empty their lives were in their endless pursuit of material things. He struck out boldly against the senselessness of war and went to jail as a protest against a government he refused to support. He stood for freedom for all men and spoke out fearlessly against those who would deny it to anyone.

He is an American to remember, a man who showed us the way to more meaningful and more honest lives. And although he often had good reason to despair, he held out hope for the improvement of mankind. His last words in *Walden* are: "There is more day to dawn. The sun is but a morning star."

It is now evident that Thoreau, who seemed hostile to others, who preferred the loneliness of the fields and the woods to the society of man, and who was outspoken in his criticism of human affairs, was not the curmudgeon he was said to be. Behind the mask was a highly sensitive person who wanted to avoid being hurt. His apparent indifference to others came from the fact that he had tried out his contemporaries and found them to be wanting. His own standards were so high that few could meet them. The world of man, according to him, is a poor place compared to the natural world where cruelty, avarice, betrayal, and vengeance are almost unknown. He made friends with the creatures of the forest. He showed his trust in them, and they reciprocated by trusting him. He was, in the fullest sense of the word, a good person. Children and animals sensed this and accepted him as one of themselves. They can pay an adult no higher tribute.

The key to understanding the complex and elusive character of this unusual man is not difficult to find. He made no secret of it but wrote it out for all to read:

Love is the wind, the tide, the waves, the sunshine. Its power is incalculable; it is many horse-power. It never ceases, it never slacks; it can move the globe without a resting-place; it can warm without fire; it can feed without meat; it can clothe without garments; it can shelter without a roof; it can make a paradise within which will dispense with a paradise without.

There was no meanness in the heart of Henry David Thoreau, no malice, no pettiness, no spite. His honesty was so apparent that no one ever questioned it. He concealed many of his best qualities, for he was not given to display. But the real value was there—and he knew it, and those he esteemed knew it, too.

It has taken a long time for the world to become aware of the real truth about this man. But now, after long neglect, he has come into his own.

Walden Pond is his memorial. Visitors from far and near go there to seek out the site where his little cabin once stood. In those quiet woods above the shore his words still resound:

The true harvest of my daily life is somewhat as intangible and indescribable as the fruits of morning or evening. It is a little star-dust caught. It is a segment of the rainbow I have clutched. . . . I waxed and grew in these intervals, as the corn grows in the night. . . . I realized what the Oriental philosophers meant by contemplation and the forsaking of works. . . . Follow your genius closely enough, and it will not fail to show you a fresh prospect every hour.

CHRONOLOGY

1817.   July 12: Henry David Thoreau is born in Concord, Massachusetts.

1818–1822.   Family moves to Chelmsford and Boston.

1823.   Returns to Concord.

1833–1837.   At Harvard.

1837.   October 22: Begins *Journal*.

1838.   Opens a private school in Concord with his brother John.

   April 11: First lecture at Concord Lyceum.

   May 2 to 17: First trip to Maine.

1839.   Meets Ellen Sewall.

   August 30 to September 13: Goes on boating trip with his brother on the Concord and Merrimack Rivers.

1840.   April: His essay "Aulus Persius Flaccus" appears in the first issue of *The Dial*. Writes "The Service."

1841.   Goes to live with the Emersons.

1842.   January 11: His brother John dies.

1843.   May 6 to December 3: In Staten Island as a tutor to the three young sons of Emerson's brother, William.

1844.   April 30: Sets fire to the Concord woods while on a fishing trip.

1845.   March: Starts to build his cabin near Walden Pond. July 4: Moves in.

1846.   July 23 or 24: Spends a night in jail for refusing to pay taxes to a government that supports slavery. August and September: Second trip to Maine woods.

1847.   September 6: Leaves Walden Pond cabin. Stays at Emerson's house again.

1848.   January 26: Gives lecture that is eventually to be called "Civil Disobedience."
"Ktaadn and the Maine Woods" appears in the *Union Magazine*. Returns to his father's house.

1849.   *A Week on the Concord and Merrimack Rivers* published.
May: "Civil Disobedience" is printed in the first and only issue of *Aesthetic Papers*.
October: First trip to Cape Cod.

1850.   Busy as a surveyor all this year.
June: Second trip to Cape Cod.
July: Goes to Fire Island, N.Y., to try to recover effects from shipwreck in which Margaret Fuller was drowned.
September: Visits Canada.

1851.   Begins his night walks. More work as a surveyor.

1853.   September 13 to 28: To the Maine woods again.

1854.   Final revisions on *Walden*.
July 4: Speaks on "Slavery in Massachusetts."
August 9: *Walden* is published.

1855.   July 4 to 18: To Cape Cod again.
Ill nearly all this year.

1856.   September: In Vermont and New Hampshire.
October: Does surveying at Eagleswood near Perth Amboy, N.J.
November 10: Visits Walt Whitman in Brooklyn.

1857.   February: Meets John Brown in Concord.
June 12 to 22: To Cape Cod again.
July 20 to August 8: To the Maine woods again.

1858.   July: Visits White Mountains.

1859.   February 3: His father dies.

May 7: John Brown is in Concord again.

October 16-18: Raid on Harpers Ferry.

October: Thoreau defends Brown's actions.

December 2: Brown is hanged.

1860. July 4: Thoreau's "The Last Days of John Brown"
is read at memorial services near North Elba, N.Y.

August: On a walking tour of western Massachusetts
and the Catskills.

November 6: Lincoln elected President.

December 3: Thoreau catches cold while outdoors
counting tree rings. The Southern states begin to
secede from the Union.

1861. February 8: Jefferson Davis becomes president of
the Confederacy.

March 4: Lincoln is inaugurated.

April 12: Fort Sumter is fired on. The Civil War
begins.

May 11 to July 10: Thoreau goes to Minnesota for
his failing health.

1862. The *Atlantic Monthly* asks him for some articles.
In a last burst of energy he prepares several earlier
pieces for publication. *Walden* is to go into a second
edition.

May 6: Thoreau dies at 9 A.M.

BIBLIOGRAPHY

The only two books of Thoreau's that were published during his lifetime are:

A Week on the Concord and Merrimack Rivers, 1849
Walden, or Life in the Woods, 1854

After his death a number of books were put together from his magazine articles and *Journal.* Among them are:

Excursions, 1863
The Maine Woods, 1864
Cape Cod, 1864
*A Yankee in Canada, with Anti-Slavery and Reform
    Papers,* 1866
Early Spring in Massachusetts, 1881
Summer, 1884
Winter, 1888
Autumn, 1892
Miscellanies, 1894

More modern works, edited on a more scholarly basis, are:
Collected Poems of Henry David Thoreau, 1943 and
    1964
    Edited by Carl Bode
The Correspondence of Henry David Thoreau, 1958
    Edited by Walter Harding and Carl Bode
The *Journal* was first issued in 1906 as part of the col-

lected works; then separately in 14 volumes in 1949. In 1962 it was reissued at a lower price in two large volumes. *The "Lost" Journal of 1840-1841* was published in 1958 under the title, *Consciousness in Concord,* edited by Perry Miller.

The best and most up-to-date biography of Thoreau is:
Walter Harding, *The Days of Henry Thoreau,* 1965.
Earlier biographies are:
Brooks Atkinson, *Henry Thoreau, The Cosmic Yankee,* 1927
Henry Seidel Canby, *Thoreau,* 1939
William Ellery Channing, *Thoreau, The Poet-Naturalist,* 1873
Joseph Wood Krutch, *Henry David Thoreau,* 1948
Milton Meltzer and Walter Harding, *A Thoreau Profile,* 1962 (illustrated)
H. A. Page (A. H. Japp), *Thoreau: His Life and Aims,* 1877 and 1968
Franklin B. Sanborn, *Henry D. Thoreau,* 1882
———, *The Life of Henry David Thoreau,* 1917 and 1968
Some of the many critical works that may be of interest are:
Reginald L. Cook, *Passage to Walden,* 1949 and 1966
Walter Harding (editor), *Thoreau, a Century of Criticism,* 1954
———, *A Thoreau Handbook,* 1959
———, *Thoreau, Man of Concord,* 1960
John H. Hicks (editor), *Thoreau in Our Season,* 1966
Sherman Paul, *The Shores of America, Thoreau's Inward Exploration,* 1958
———, *Thoreau: A Collection of Critical Essays,* 1962
James Lyndon Shanley, *The Making of Walden,* 1957
A useful one-volume edition of selections from Thoreau's writings is:
The Portable Thoreau, 1947, edited by Carl Bode.

INDEX

177

ABOUT THE AUTHOR

Philip Van Doren Stern is the author or editor of more than fifty books on subjects that range from the Model T Ford to secret missions of the Civil War. Many of Mr. Stern's books deal with nineteenth-century American history and literature, and Henry David Thoreau has long been one of his special interests. He is the editor of *The Annotated Walden*, a detailed examination of Thoreau's most famous book.

Mr. Stern was born in Wyalusing, Pennsylvania, and educated at Rutgers, which conferred on him the honorary degree of Doctor of Letters. He is also a former Guggenheim fellow and has worked in advertising and as a book designer and editor. His interests, which are reflected, of course, in many of his books, include art, travel, and photography. Mr. Stern now lives and writes in Norwalk, Connecticut.